MW01596728

Pet Care Guide

*For Tailwaggin' Fun
and Purrfect Health*

Robert Uherka
Lauren Scott

RJLA, Inc.
ISBN # 0-9653148-2-0

Contributing editors
  Jennifer Coburn
  O'Neal Scott
Graphic Illustrators
  Nicole Scott
  Jason Clemens
  Lynda B. Nario
Cover Photography
  Brian Bork

ISBN # 0-9653148-2-0

*Attention animal welfare groups, clubs, charitable organizations
and all other interested parties. PetPages™ is available at special
quantity discounts and makes for an effective fund raising product.
Please call for more information.*

<u>Dedication</u>

*To the magical, precious, furry, four-legged angels
that bless us each day with lessons, love, and
laughter.*

CONTENTS

To Our Readers:

This book was written with the sincerest desire to enrich the lives of pets and their owners. For many of us, pets are an integral part of our lives. They are certainly considered members of our families. The challenge today is finding places to go and things to do that will allow pet parents to include their beloved pet. The goal of this book is to provide pet owners with an abundance of ideas and ways to involve their pet in activities they both can enjoy. In addition, we wanted you, the pet owner, to have valuable pet care information and practical tips to insure your pet receives the best possible care. We know that pets who receive proper care and attention are happier and happier pets mean happier parents.

Pet ownership is all about care, love, and companionship. With the help of this book, pet owners can strengthen their "friendship" with their pet by adding fun and adventure to their pet care routine.

We are interested in any additional ideas or suggestions that you may have. What you share with us we can share with thousands of pet owners striving to enrich the lives of their pets.

Have fun!

Chapter 1

Places to Go

It's time to get out and have some fun with your furry friend. Many pet owners are unaware of the number of great places you can take your pet. They are actually welcome in lots of outdoor areas. Contact your local and county parks departments for details regarding pets. Most parks will require that dogs be kept on leashes. However, there is a growing trend toward "dog" parks that provide fenced off-leash areas. These are wonderful for dogs who really like to run. Once you've decided on your destination, below are some suggestions to ensure a safe and fun outing.

- Be sure your pet is in good health and has current vaccinations.
- Pick up after your pet.
- Have a well mannered pet (not aggressive). Your pet should know basic obedience commands such as come,

sit-stay, and down-stay.
- Keep your pet on leash at all times.
- Don't allow your pet to bother others.
- Bring pet treats, chew toys, water & bowls.
- Check your pet for fleas, ticks, burrs, and other hazards.
- Never take your pet out of your home without some form of identification. You normally don't go anywhere without your ID, neither should your pet.

Social Skills

Wherever you take your pet, you will most likely encounter other dogs and their owners. In general, most dogs behave when they meet on neutral ground. However, always exercise caution when you or your pet meet a new dog. Here are a few tips to help avoid possible dog fights.

Tips on Avoiding Dog Fights

- Keep your dog on a leash.
- As you approach other leashed dogs, be sure there is ample room between them.
- Don't approach dogs without their owner's permission.
- Even with permission, approach a new dog slowly and cautiously.

How to Break Up a Dog Fight

- Respond quickly, but do not endanger your safety.
- Make a loud noise to distract dogs, or douse them both with water.
- Do not get in the middle of the fight or even close to the fighting dogs - keep a safe distance or you may be accidentally bitten.
- If your dog is wounded in a fight, call your veterinarian immediately.
- Be sure to exchange name, address, and phone number information with the other pet owner.

Beaches/Lakes

Some dogs absolutely love to swim and there are others that are less than thrilled at the thought of getting wet. DO NOT ASSUME ALL DOGS KNOW HOW TO SWIM. Some pets may panic. Be prepared to assist if your pet seems unsure. With some support and encouragement from you, a willing pet will quickly catch on. For those pets that will fetch, throwing a tennis ball or any other floatable toy out in the water is great fun and exercise. Watch for any signs of fatigue. Dogs can drown from exhaustion. Be sure that your pet has a safe path into the water. Slippery rocks, broken glass, fallen branches, or other sharp objects in or around water's edge can be extremely hazardous. Also, be aware that many of these objects could be out of eyesight, just below the water's surface. Bring fresh water for pet to drink. Try to discourage your pet from drinking lake, stream, and salt water. There are parasites and bacteria found in these water sources that my be harmful to your pet.

TIP: Always bring fresh water for your pet. Parasites and bacteria found in lakes, streams, and salt water can be harmful to your pet.

Water Tips

- Be careful of strong currents or riptides.
- Never throw or frighten dog into water.
- Use specially formulated pet sunscreen on dogs with light-colored hair in the areas of their nose and ears, where the hair is thin and the skin is more exposed (pets are subject to sunburns and skin cancer).
- Rocky or steep embankments can be dangerous or hard for tired pets.
- Some dogs may be frightened by large waves found on ocean beaches but are fine with calmer waters such as lakes and streams. Be sensitive to their fears.

Hiking

Hiking with your pet is wonderful exercise and fun for you and your pet. Not only will your pet enjoy the adventure of new sights and smells, but you'll enjoy watching his enthusiasm. Who knows what new things you'll discover by watching him uncover treasures in the brush.

As with any exercise, begin slowly allowing your pet to gradually increase his stamina. Monitor the distance of the hike. You know your pet's health and how far he can go. Don't push past that point or you may end up carrying him back. If he shows signs of tiring - stop! Be sure that you bring plenty of water for him to drink throughout the hike. On warm days, be sure to rest in shady spots. Don't let pets overheat, they depend on you to slow them down. Pets don't realize that if they keep running, they'll drop from exhaustion. If your pet does overheat, you need to cool him down immediately. Find shade and give him water. If possible, submerge him in water. See EMERGENCY SECTION for what to do for heat stroke.

Remember pets can suffer from sore muscles and joints from overdoing it, just like us. If you notice your pet moving slowly the next day, check with your veterinarian just to be safe. If he has sore muscles, encourage your pet to do a little stretching, take a short walk, and pamper him with a gentle massage, he will love you for it!

TIP:
As with any exercise, begin slowly allowing your pet to gradually increase his stamina. Pets can suffer form sore muscles and joints too!

Keep your pet safe under watchful care. Always keep pet in sight even in areas where pets are allowed off leash. There are many possible dangers like poisonous snakes, insects, traffic, and animals that could harm your pet.

You have hiking boots, now your pet can too. For pet's comfort, you may want to purchase dog boots. It sounds funny but they really make a difference. Your pet will get used to them and appreciate them. If your pet prefers to rough it, be sure to check his feet regularly for cracks, blisters, or any debris that may be caught between toes. Frequent checks are especially important if you are hiking on rough terrain with sharp rocks, sticks, or pine cones. Even the most experienced dog can develop tender paws.

Backpacks are available for dogs. Before purchasing one for your pet, think about the following. Is your dog large enough to carry one and is he in shape to take on the additional weight? Backpacks may be too much for many small dogs. Consult your veterinarian if you have any questions. If you decide to use a dog backpack, be careful not to overload it to the point of stressing your dog's back and muscles. Dogs carrying the extra weight can overexert themselves and end up with sore muscles or possible injuries.

While hiking, be on the lookout for poison oak. Although it may not bother your pet, he can bring it back to you, your home, and family. By gathering the itchy oils on his fur, you may unknowingly pet the oils onto your skin. A bath after hiking in areas that may contain poison oak is recommended.

At the conclusion of your hike, check your pet for ticks, fleas, foxtail, scratches, or any other problems.

Hiking Tips

- For pet's safety, don't allow pets to interact with wildlife.
- Depending on the length of the hike, bring snacks or food for your pet.
- Bring water for your pet. Discourage pet from drinking water from lakes or streams. These water sources may contain harmful bacteria.
- Check pet's feet frequently for any soreness.
- Monitor pet's pace, allow time for rest and water as needed.

Camping Tips

For the safety of your pet, he should sleep in the tent with you. Most camp sites will require it. Tying pets up outside leaves them vulnerable to wild animals. He may also escape and get lost. After all, why do you think they call them pup tents?

For the comfort of your pet, consider bringing a mat or two for him to lay on inside and outside of the tent. Many camp-sites are either rocky or bare dirt. Very seldom do you find a grassy shady spot for Rover to rollover!

Safety tips for camping:

1. Groom your dog every night. Check around eyes and ears, and between toes. Run your fingers through its fur and comb off any burrs, ticks, or seeds.

2. Keep your dog away from wild animals. Even harmless looking animals can carry deadly diseases.

3. Pay attention to your dog's body tempature. Heat stroke in the sun or hypothermia in the cold can happen very sud denly.

4. Carry a first-aid kit. See our tips on first-aid kits in chapter five.

5. Call ahead to the camping area and ask about any plant or animal hazards. Avoiding problems is easier when you know what they are.

6. Prevent your dog from drinking from natural water sources. Dogs are susceptible to Giardia and other water parasistes.

Restaurants

Yes, believe it or not, many cities do allow pets in outdoor dining areas. On nice days, this is a wonderful way for you to include your pet. While you're dining, your pet can relax and do a little people watching. Before heading out to your favor-ite restaurant with your pet, be sure to give them a call and ask if your "well-mannered" dog is welcome in their outdoor dining area. The emphasis here is on "well-mannered". Dogs with bad manners will NOT be welcome at any restaurant and will probably cause a restaurant to change its pet friendly policy. So, please be sure that Sparky is obedience trained. Here are a few additional tips to make your dining excursion more enjoyable.

Dining Tips

- Bring a rawhide chew or favorite toy to occupy pet while you're dining.
- Only bring pets that will sit or lay quietly at the table.
- Pets should be well-mannered and not disturb other diners.
- Bring a water bowl for your pet, don't expect the restaurant to provide one.

Be sure to let management know that you appreciate the opportunity to bring your favorite pal.

Activity Forms

For your convenience we've included blank "Activity Forms" in the back of the book to document your adventures. You'll find forms for favorite outings to parks, trails, and such, as well as, restauarant and note forms. Here's an example of a completed form. We'd love to hear about your adventures. How do you rate your local parks? What are your favorite spots? Are there special places you and your four-legged buddy go that we may be able to share with other pet owners in possible future publications? Please share your thoughts by writing to us at 9921 Carmel Mountain Road #303, San Diego, California 92129.

See next page for a sample....

Activity Notes:

Date: ___9-22-97___

Pooch Park

Name of Location

Elmdale (Northwest of Hwy 8)

City or Area

☒Park   ☐Trail   ☐Beach   ☐Other _____

What would you rate this location? ___5___
(1-Ho hum, 5-Great) Meaning - *Would you go
back?*

Things we did: _____ *Brought picnic lunch
and treats for Bailey and Corky.
Jogged around the park, played with the
frisbee and the tennis balls. Great open
space!*

SAMPLE

Likes: _____ *Other dogs to play with, running
trail, lots of parking, no busy streets, lots
of grassy areas to play on, dogs just loved
it. Definitely will want to go back to it.*

Special
Notes:
*15 minutes from house. Take
jacket next time, it gets breezy in
the afternoon. Bring towels, dogs
love to play in the pond.*

Chapter 2

Exercise & Play

To keep your pet happy and healthy, daily exercise and play is a must. Being active with your pet is good for both of you. This is your time to bond, relax, exercise, and have fun with your pet on a daily basis. Pick an activity that you both can enjoy. This time with you will become the highlight of your pet's day. Pets are reliable and enthusiastic playmates. Unlike most people, he'll look forward to your exercise routine.

Without a daily exercise routine, pets become bored and that's when trouble begins. Your pet will look for something to occupy his time and mind. For dogs, this may end up being barking, digging, chewing, or finding ways to escape. A bored cat may scratch, climb, or yowl.

The type and amount of exercise will depend on you and your pet's interest, age, and health. You and your pet should enjoy the activity. Don't force a pet to participate in something he clearly doesn't like. Talk with your veterinarian about your pet's health with respect to an exercise plan. This is especially important for aging or overweight pets.

Just like aerobics, begin your exercise routine with an easy warm up and end with a cool down. If possible, try to set aside the same time every day for your pet, they love routine. Avoid exercising one hour before or after meals.

NOTE:
Without daily exercise, pets become bored and that's when trouble begins. The type of exercise will depend on your pet's interest, age and health.

Begin exercise slowly. Keep an eye on your pet and be prepared to stop if he appears tired or out of breath. He may slow down, pant heavily, or even refuse to move. He's telling you — STOP, I'm pooped! Don't overdo it. Pets will experience sore, stiff muscles too.

If you'll be exercising when it's dark, be sure that you and your pet are visible. Reflective collars and vests are available for pets.

What to do when you can't be there . . .

There will be times when, for whatever reason, you won't be able to do your daily exercise with your pet and that's okay. Just plan for someone else to fill in for you. This may be a neighbor, friend, pet sitter, or even pet daycare. Your pet will miss you, but will be appreciative of the ongoing routine and care.

Pet sitters are available to do daily stops at your home to walk, play, or feed your pet. This is wonderful for times when you're not feeling well, tied up at work, or simply unable to exercise your pet.

Another alternative is pet daycare. This is now available in many cities. Owners drop their pets off for a day filled with fun and companionship. Depending on the daycare center, it may offer swimming, indoor and/or outdoor play, scheduled exercise time, and rest. Some centers even offer obedience training. Use the same care as selecting any petcare visit and ask questions.

The next best playmate is another dog or cat for your pet to play with when you're unavailable. Pets with partners are happier, healthier, and live longer. A playmate helps lighten the owner's load. Two can play, groom, rest, and explore. It brings new life to the current pet. If adding another pet just isn't possible, consider a plan where your pet can get together with a compatible pet friend. This may mean that you drop Sparky off at your friend's house to play with her friend Skippy.

Home Alone Pets

Being left alone for eight to ten hours each day can get lonely for a pet. And, boredom usually spells trouble. Create diversions, leave your pet with entertaining toys. When you're home, make sure your pet gets plenty of play and exercise with you.

Tips for Indoor Pets

- Establish a regular routine for morning and evening.
- Include exercise in daily schedule.
- Spend quality time with your pet.
- Make sure area where you're leaving pet is safe.
- Help make home comfortable for your pet, provide a comfortable bed, leave a radio or TV on to keep pet company, and don't forget safe toys.
- For dogs, hire a dog-walking service, or a dog-loving neighbor, to break up your dog's day with a visit and some exercise.
- Adopt a second pet.
- Give your pet an interesting outdoor view. (Pets like to watch activity: squirrels, birds, people, etc.)
- Phone home and leave messages for pets.
- For dogs, limit crate time to three or four hours a day (except at bedtime).

■   Don't make a big deal over departures and arrivals.

Tips for Outside Dogs

Dogs can live outside, but are happiest when they're inside with their pack (you). If you have an outdoor dog, he can be eased into the indoor life with proper training.

Don't expel a dog to the outside because of a problem behavior. Instead, get proper training for your pet. Most problems stem from boredom. Your dog will be just as bored in the yard as he was in the house, now, you'll just have a new set of outdoor behavior problems like barking, digging, chewing, etc.

If your dog enjoys the outdoors and it works with your lifestyle, keep him an outward hound. But keep him healthy and happy by providing proper shelter and family interaction. Your dog should have a shaded area, shelter with comfortable, clean bedding, fresh water, and plenty of daily exercise and playtime with you. Don't assume that your pet will get adequate exercise on his own left in the yard. Most likely he will not. Plan daily exercise and play time with your pet. Consider having a friend, neighbor, or pet sitter take your pet out for midday walks. Be sure that your pet has toys to occupy his time. Make sure your yard has no escape routes or dangerous objects. Be prepared to relocate your pet indoors when weather is extreme.

Also be aware that pet theft is a possibility from yards, especially for purebred dogs. A tall fence with locked gates is your best bet against pet theft if you choose to have your pet outside.

Dog Exercise

Begin any exercise program slowly and gradually increase the duration or difficulty. Be sensitive to the weather for outdoor activities. Avoid activities in extreme weather. During hot months, plan exercise in early or late day when it's cooler. Always have plenty of water available and take breaks. And don't forget pet sunscreen for light-colored pets. Their sensitive noses and ears will burn on sunny days.

Exercise with your dog will be safer and much more enjoyable if your pet is obedience trained. It's not fun to walk a dog who's pulling you down the street. It will be important that your pet know the basics like sit, stay, come, and heel.

TIP:
Exercise with your dog will be safer and much more enjoyable, if your pet knows the basic obedience training like sit, stay, come, and heel.

Walking

There isn't a dog alive who doesn't enjoy a walk with his best friend. However, for you to share the enjoyment, your pet must know how to heel (walk at your side with no pulling on the leash). If he doesn't know how to heel, this would be a good time to incorporate a little training into the walk. A brisk twenty-minute walk two times a day will satisfy most pet's exercise needs.

Jogging

Although jogging may be your chosen form of exercise, it may or may not be a good choice for your pet. Talk with your veterinarian before jogging, it is not recommended for small breeds, aging pets, or pets with joint problems. Never force a dog to run. Exercise caution on warm days. Hot or rough surfaces can cause blisters or cracked pads. Be sure to check your pet's paws frequently and have plenty of fresh water available for him.

Biking with dog

This is one of the most strenuous activities for a dog because it requires him to maintain a constant pace to keep up with you. To ensure that your pet is biking material, check with your veterinarian before beginning a biking program. Bike at a speed that allows your dog to trot rather than run. Check your pet's paws frequently for blisters or cracked pads. Avoid biking with your pet on hot days. Stop for water breaks.

Swimming

Swimming is a terrific form of exercise for dogs. This is especially true for older dogs or dogs with joint problems. However, not all dogs will enjoy or even like the idea of getting wet. Try it and see if your pal takes to the water. Go slow, your pet may need some help and encouragement figuring out the dog paddle. But with a little patience and practice, most dogs will quickly catch on. Be sure to watch for signs of tiring or you may find yourself swimming out to rescue a drowning dog. If your dog likes to retrieve, consider bringing tennis balls or other floatable toys to toss in the water. Check out the water and play area for safety before allowing your pet to swim. Is the water clean and safe from toxins? Is there a safe path in and out of the water?

Discourage pet from drinking water found in lakes, streams, and salt water. Parasites and bacteria found in these bodies of water can be harmful. Instead, bring fresh water from home for your pet to drink.

Pool Proof Your Dog

If your dog has access to a swimming pool, make sure she has an easy way out such as steps or a slanted board. Bring your dog in the pool and show her how to get out. Again, do not assume that she will figure it out on her own.

For pets that are less sure of the water, there are dog life vests available. These are especially good for boaters who take their pets or for pets that just don't swim well.

Fetch or Catch

A game of fetch is great for owners who want to relax while their pet exercises. This activity assumes that your pet has been taught to return the thrown object. Some pets will automatically retrieve the object with little training. Most pets will probably require some training. Once trained, this is an excellent outlet for energy and dogs love it. Experiment with your pet to figure out what is his favorite item to fetch or catch. Some favorites include tennis balls, Kongs™ (bee-hive shaped rubber toy that bounces erratically when thrown), and Frisbees™. For long distance throws, use a tennis racket to hit the tennis ball or the Original Fetchball™ Scoop. Always play on soft grassy areas. Asphalt or concrete can be hard on a pet's feet.

TIP: For long distance throws, use a tennis racket to hit the ball. Always play on soft grassy areas. Asphalt or concrete can be hard on a pet's feet.

Dog Play

Okay, so your pet is exercised and rested. Now it's time for fun. Playtime for your pet may or may not include you. His preference would be to have you participate. But for those times you aren't there to play, provide your pet with toys and activities that will keep him occupied. The bottom line is to have fun, be creative, and get silly with your pet. Trust me, he'll love it!

Outdoor Pets

Liven up a boring backyard by creating a playground for your pet. Think about your pet and what he'd like to do during the day. If he's a digger, put in a sandbox for him. Bury some of his favorite toys in the sand. If your yard is somewhat se-cluded, maybe a ramp leading up to a perch with a view would satisfy his curiosity and allow him to see activity outside his yard. Cut out a peek-hole in the fence that would allow a view but no escapes or biting passersby. A tire (no steel belt tires) hanging from a tree may be a good chew or tug toy for a large dog. Is your dog a leaper or jumper? Then maybe a series of hurdles could prepare him for agility competition. Even a large empty box could provide hours of entertainment. Invite another dog friend to spend the day. Encourage your pet to use his hunting skills by hiding treats or toys in the yard.

Dog Play Groups

For a really special treat, get your pet together with a number of his other canine pals for some free play. The meeting can take place at a home with a yard or a public area that preferably allows pets off leash. Doing this on a regular basis is a lot of fun for the dogs and spectators. The dogs will form friendships with each other and will really look forward to the group session. Be prepared for an enthusiastic display of play skills as they race, chase, roll, tumble, jump, and bark. Be mindful of toy possessiveness. It may be better not to bring toys if they tend to fight over them. Or, bring enough toys so that each pet has one. Guaranteed, you will leave with one happy pup.

Hide and Seek

Remember how much fun you used to have playing hide and seek? Well, now you can relive childhood memories with your four legged kid(s) and have just as much fun today. Simply put your pet in a "sit-stay" and head for a hiding place. Then give your pet the "okay" signal to look for you. Lavish your pet with praise when she finds you. Start off with easy hiding spots so that your pet gets the hang of the game. This can be played inside or outside. Another twist is to hide treats or special toys and let your pet find them. Be sure to vary the pattern so it's a challenge.

Tracking

For dogs that like to use their noses, tracking is lots of fun. Begin by putting your pet in a "sit-stay" away from the tracking area. She may watch from a distance. Then take a treat your pet likes (cheese or hot-dogs work well), rub a little on your shoes, and scuff a path through the grass. Periodically drop a little piece of the treat along the path. Go back and take your pet to the start of the laid track, and encourage her to follow the track. Using her nose, she'll follow the track and collect the treat rewards along the way. As she becomes better, the track can become longer and more erratic.

Homemade Toys

Some of the best toys come from the grocery store. Empty paper grocery bags, cardboard tubes from paper towels or giftwrap (especially after you shout the ta-dooo, ta-dooo rebel yell through them), and empty plastic milk containers. Granted, these are short-lived "toys" but, for that brief moment your pet will be captivated by the excitement of something new and different. Basically, if you begin the play and show an interest in whatever the toy, your pet will want to be involved. No self-respecting pet turns down an opportunity to play.

Toys

There are wide varieties of toys available for dogs. As with children's toys, keep safety in mind as you purchase toys for your pet. So, let's say you've bought a large assortment of toys. They're scattered all over your home and your pet seems totally bored with all of them. What can you do? Add some interest back into these current toys. First, pick them all up and put them in a basket or box. As you do this, undoubtedly your pet will wonder what you're doing and where you're going with his possessions. Already his toys are taking on new meaning. Next, allow your pet to select one or two toys from the container. Each day put back the toys and allow him to select his toys for the day. This rotation of toys will help minimize toy boredom. Another important part of this process is your handling of the toys. If you're paying attention to his toys, then so will he. Pets like toys that have their owner's scent on them.

TIP: Rotating toys will help minimize toy boredom. If you pay attention to their toys, then so will they. Pets like their owner's scent on their toys.

Another option is to take sterilized dog bones, Kongs™, or Nylabones™ (with holes drilled in them) and stuff them with a favorite treat like peanut butter or cheese. Your dog will spend hours chewing on these tasty toys.

Dog Tricks

Teaching a dog tricks can be enjoyable for pet and owner. Pets love to please their owner. Training a pet to learn new tricks requires patience, consistency, and rewards. Think about what new fun trick you can teach your pet. Whether it's shaking paws, fetching the newspaper, or barking on command, remember to have fun, this is play time.

Special Report From Barkin' Bailey

Our roving reporter, Barkin' Bailey, comes to us from a local park, where she's talking with fellow canines about their favorite activities.

Well Bailey . . .

"HELLO EVERYONE!!! Barkin' Bailey here. I put my nose to the ground to find out what makes a dog's tail wag.

"There are many pleasures in life that are treasured by dogs. Most involve their owners. I had an opportunity to interview a few lucky pooches here at the park. Here's what they had to say . . .

"Taylor, a golden retriever mix, explains indoor hide and seek: *It's silly, but it's so much fun. I sit while my companion hides. When I hear a tiny 'O.K.!' I'm off to find the secret hiding spot. This is where my keen senses are challenged. My ears listen for movement or breathing, my eyes are quick to see the sight of my friend, and my nose — oh, how I sniff and sniff. Sometimes I can find the secret hiding place only using my sense of smell. (NO, my friend is not stinky! I just know her scent.) When I find her, we jump and shout and run around. Sometimes this turns into a fun game of tag. We get all excited and woofy. Ohhh, I get all giggly, wiggly just thinking about it.*

Bowie, a park regular, enjoys the chance to meet and play with other dogs of all sizes, shapes and breeds. (Although, Bowie has been known to *borrow* toys from other dogs.)

Thor, a sensitive German Shepherd, says his favorite activity is the quiet time spent relaxing with his owner and friend, Chris. Thor's voice, filling with love and contentment, says, *"Those quiet moments really make a difference. To a dog, nothing is more important than being with the pack."*

Bomber, an athletic Old Danish Pointer, joyfully states, *"I'd go everywhere if I could! Lately I've even enjoyed going to restaurants around the area. I try to be very good and lay by the table, but sometimes I get excited with all the sights, smells, and sounds. One time the chef gave me a special treat. It was delicious!"*

Corky, an energetic terrier mix, likes walks, morning, noon, or night — anytime is right. *"Most of my friends prefer several frequent walks a day, although even one long walk is nice."*

Tawny, a sweet, loveable Sharpei, enjoys "A gentle massage and brushing session . . . sigh." He says, *"It's great for getting rid of stress."*

Bernie, a big St. Bernard, likes *"A game of chase! Balls, Frisbees, cats, cars . . . oops . . . the last two aren't allowed, but some dogs get carried away when they are not given any direction or toys to play with. It is also advisable to make sure it is a safe area to run openly. Some dogs say they even bring them back to be thrown again (humans call it retrieving)."*

"Lastly, but most importantly — communication. Everyone polled agrees that this is the hardest to establish, but that it makes such a difference in their relationships with humans.

Max, a beautiful Rottweiler, says, *"Humans just don't know dog language and theirs is so complicated! Sometimes it sounds like blah blah blah, Max, blah, blah, blah. But with consistent repetition, my companion now understands my communication for a walk, going out to do duties, dinner, snacks, playtime, and alert — stranger approaching. In turn, I can proudly say my human vocabulary is up to 27 words. We get along so well when we understand each other."* This is strongly encouraged for everyone!

"There are differences in choices of activities when you bring age into the equation. Puppies all want the same things — eat, play, bite everything (they're teething), and sleep. This pattern is repeated over and over, day and night.

"On the other hand, senior dogs usually voice an opinion for slower paced activities."

Cardiff, a distinguished older terrier, had this great idea for senior dogs. She enjoys elderly neighbors and nursing homes. These folks are gentle with her, and they like to talk to her and pet her. Little kids are just too frisky and unpredictable for her to keep up with; she has gotten hurt in the past. Besides, Muffin says, *"it does so much for the people."* She's heard it said that dogs have been known to give joy and purpose to people's lives, and they actually live longer.

"When breed and personality are considered, there are so many more activities that are loved by some and others would just as soon not do. Water is a good example of this. Some dogs just do not like water — especially baths. Others heard the word water and ears shot up A very rambunctious chocolate Labrador, Dakota, LOVES the water. He'll happily participate in boating, swimming, fetching toys thrown in the water, running on the shore, playing in a child's pool, or even playing in the sprinklers. All this talk about playing in the water left a lot of tails wagging.

"Just like people, dogs have their own personality, likes, and dislikes. Some dogs are real outdoorsy, you know, frontier dogs. They like to hike, camp, travel, and explore. Then there are the couch potatoes who prefer the comfort and predictability of home. You'll find them relaxing in their favorite spot.

"Clubs like hunting, tracking, agility, Frisbee, and trail were mentioned. There are so many clubs and new ones are forming all the time. What's so great is how much fun these groups are! Try one and see. If it doesn't thrill you, try another club. The dogs who were members couldn't say enough good things about them.

"That's about it here at the park! Companions, please use this as a reference to get started with 'dog friendly' activities. Customize it for both you and your dog's pleasure. If you come up with a great tail wagging idea, please write the editors of this book and they may be able to print it in a future publication.

"Signing off, this is Barkin' Bailey, for the PetPages."

Cat Play

Yes, cats are pretty independent and generally don't require a lot of our attention. But they really do like to play, some just may not realize it. Playtime is especially important for indoor cats. An outdoor cat has opportunities all day to hunt and play.

Playtime for a cat is just another form of hunting. You may notice that your cat has a ground or air hunt preference. If so, then your task is to think like a bird or a mouse.

Cat Play Rules

1) Cats only play when they want to play. You can try coaxing them, but don't be disappointed if she doesn't go for it.

2) Cats have short attention spans. Play time will probably last 10 to 20 minutes.

3) Beware of very fast and sharp claws that may accidentally catch you.

4) Never leave string, yarn, or thread out unattended. Cats can become entangled in it and harm themselves. Also, it is very dangerous if the string is ingested, the barbs on a cat's tongues do not allow it to spit the string out.

Hide & Seek

This is not for everyone. But, there are some unique kitties out there that really do participate in a rollicking game of hide and seek. You run and hide, kitty chases, and you pop out from your hiding spot as she careens closer. This is fast-paced. She won't be waiting for you to carefully select your hiding place. She'll be hot on your trail as you scurry around the corner. So you've got to be fast.

Chase me, Chase Me

Every now and then your cat may enjoy a good chase, that is, you chasing her, much like how litter-mates would chase each other about the room. A little squeal or "boo" sound-effect is optional as you almost catch her. The objective is to get close, but not catch her. Let her be the victor.

Catch the Light

In a dimly lit area, turn on flashlight and watch kitty try to catch the light as it moves around the room. You may want to begin this game with a pencil flashlight.

Toys

Think of safety first. No toys with loose, sharp parts that may poke, cut, or be swallowed.

Fishing

Another cat favorite looks similar to a fishing pole with a string and feathers attached on the end. This works well as a high flyin' bird or when darted along the floor.

Paper

Be creative and think paper. Cats love little paper balls to bat around the floor. They like piles of newspapers spread out and tented up. Biting corners of envelopes is another pastime. Empty paper grocery bags laid on their side always offers some mystery to a cat. This is especially true if she hears something gently tapping on the side of that bag (just don't let her know it's you). Moving paper or still, wherever there is paper, there will mostly likely be a cat sitting in the midst of it.

Boxes

Empty boxes capture the attention and curiosity of most cats. Tossing a small ball or cork in the box will add further interest to a cat. After the mystery of the box is solved, you'll probably find your cat happily catching a nap in the new "hiding" place.

> TIP:
> Playtime for a cat is just another form of hunting. Notice if your cat has a ground or air hunt preference. If so, your task is to think like a bird or a mouse.

Bunny Kick Toys

Once a cat catches its prey, it will roll over on its back while holding its prey against its stomach and bunny kick it. Your cat may enjoy bunny kicking a tennis ball, a stuffed sock (particularly if it's stuffed with catnip), or any small soft stuffed object the size of a mouse or bird.

Ball Games

Another spin on the hunt game for kitty is to roll any small object for her to chase. The key here is to roll the object away from her, not toward her. The game is to think like an itty-bitty mouse running and hiding from your big, scary cat. Proven rollable objects that have met cats' expectations are ping-pong balls, plastic golf balls, empty plastic thread spools, small plastic egg-shaped containers, plastic lemons, rollable nuts, and wine corks.

Movie Matinees

Yes, there are cats that enjoy a good video. There are even videos on the market that are specifically made for cats. Try it, see if your cat isn't mesmerized. No popcorn necessary. This is a great thing to leave on for kitty when she's alone.

Catnip

Catnip, the recreational drug for cats, can be grown or purchased in pet stores. The fresher the better. Intoxicated cats may become mellow, sleepy, playful, feisty, or content. Many toys are available with catnip. They will need to be replaced periodically as they lose their "nip" appeal.

Playground

Provide your cat with a "playground." This may include objects to climb, scratch, high places to hide, or catwalks. These can be purchased or made.

Let The Sun Shine In

Naps in the sun are vital to a cats happiness. A sunny window view is ideal. Place a chair or table in front of the window so that kitty can enjoy her nap site. Window sill mounts are also available to accommodate cat perches. Never leave windows open without screens, cats can fall out.

Clubs & Activities

Are you interested in a cat group or a dog group? Purebred or mixed breed? Do you want to participate or would you rather be a spectator? Whatever your interest, there's bound to be a group just for you. This section lists clubs and activities available to pet owners, along with a national contact for each activity. This contact may be used to find out more about that specific activity or as a resource to locate local clubs in your area. Please include a self addressed stamped envelope with your correspondence with these groups. Most groups are non-profit organizations and will appreciate the postage savings. As people continue to become more social with their pets, the number of and types of groups continue to grow as well. Get involved, you and your pet will love it.

Dog Clubs & Activities

Dog Shows (Breed Shows)

The purpose of dog shows is to evaluate purebred, registered dogs as to how well they compare with written breed standards. The standards include size, color, temperament, proportion, structure, and movement. In essence, they are looking for the ideal dog to represent that breed. Spayed or neutered pets are not allowed. For more information, contact the following clubs.

American Kennel Club
5580 Centerview Drive
Suite 200
Raleigh, NC 27606
919-233-9767

United Kennel Club
100 East Kilgore Road
Kalamazoo, MI 49001-5598
616-343-9020

Obedience Trials

Obedience trials test a dog's ability to perform a set of exercises. The dog's appearance is not judged. Exercises that are judged include the ability to heel on-lead and off-lead, stand for examination, come when called, and sit and lie down on command. Advanced exercises include: jump and retrieve on-command, hand signals, and the ability to recognize handler's scent on articles. Contact the following clubs for more information regarding obedience trails.

American Kennel Club
5580 Centerview Drive
Suite 200
Raleigh, NC 27606
919-233-9767

United Kennel Club
100 East Kilgore Road
Kalamazoo, MI 49001-5598
616-343-9020

American Mixed Breed Obedience Registration
P.O. Box 7841
Rockford, IL 61126-7841
815-874-2909

Mixed Breed Dog Club of America
13884 State Rt 104
Lucasville, OH 45648-8586
614-259-3941

AKC Junior Showmanship

Junior Showmanship is for young handlers between the ages of
10 and 18 years old. They are judged on their handling
abilities and skills. The dog is not judged. Contact the AKC
for more information.

American Kennel Club
5580 Centerview Drive
Suite 200
Raleigh, NC 27606
919-233-9767

AKC Canine Good Citizen Test

This test is open to pure and mixed breed dogs. The purpose is
to demonstrate that the pet has good manners. Each dog is
judged individually on a set of ten exercises. It is not competitive. The pet receives a certificate for passing the test. Below
is the list of exercises required in the CGC test.

1) The dog should allow a friendly stranger to approach and
    speak with the handler. The dog shouldn't shy away or act
    aggressively.

2) The dog should sit politely for petting from a friendly

stranger.

3) Appearance and grooming. The dog should allow the evaluator to brush or comb him and examine his ears and front feet.

4) Walk on a loose lead. The handler stays in control while taking dog through a series of turns and stops.

5) The dog politely walks through a crowd without straining or pulling on leash.

6) The dog should sit and down on command, then stay in place.

7) The dog should come when called.

8) Reaction to another dog. The dog must show no more than casual interest in approaching dog and handler as they stop and continue past.

9) Reaction to distractions tests dog's confidence. The dog mustn't panic, bark, or respond aggressively to distraction.

10) Dog must behave (no barking, whining, etc.) when left alone with someone else.

Any group, club, or dog enthusiast may organize this event. The AKC will provide information and test kits for all interested parties. Contact the AKC for details.

American Kennel Club
Attn: CGC
5580 Centerview Drive
Suite 200
Raleigh, NC 27606
212-696-8322

Herding

A variety of herding tests and trials exist. Ducks, sheep, or cattle are used in the herding exercises. To learn more about herding, contact the following groups.

American Herding Breed Association
3767 W. 126th St
Cleveland, OH 44111
216-941-6330

American Kennel Club
5580 Centerview Drive
Suite 200
Raleigh, NC 27606
919-233-9767

United States Border Collie Handlers' Association
Rt. 14A
Crawford, TX 76638

Australian Shepherd Club of America
6091 E. Hwy. 21
Bryan, TX 77803-9652
409-778-1082

Agility Trials

This sport is as much fun to watch as it is to participate. It's basically an obstacle course for dogs that's judged on speed and accuracy. The obstacle course includes jumping hurdles, running through tunnels, scaling ramps, crossing a narrow raised dog walk, traversing a see-saw, and weaving through poles. The course is completed with the dog off-leash and the handler beside them. It's an exciting activity that blends training and athletic ability. Contact these groups for more information.

US Dog Agility Association
PO Box 850955
Richardson, TX 75085-0955
214-231-9700

American Kennel Club
5580 Centerview Drive
Suite 200

Raleigh, NC 27606
919-233-9767

United Kennel Club
100 East Kilgore Road
Kalamazoo, MI 49001-5598
616-343-9020

National Committee for Dog Agility
401 Bluemont Circle
Manhattan, KS 66502
916-966-5287

Mixed Breed Dog Club of America
13884 State Rt 104
Lucasville, OH 45648-8586
614-259-3941

North American Agility Council
HCR 2, Box 277
St. Maries, ID 83861
208-689-3803

Australian Shepherd Club of America
6091 East State Hwy 21
Bryan, TX 77803-9652
409-778-1082

Field Trials & Hunting Clubs

Field Trials and Hunting Tests demonstrate a dog's ability to
perform in the field. This may include pointing, flushing
birds, retrieving, tracking, or style. Dogs are judged against
standards, they do not compete against each other. Contact
these groups for more information.

American Kennel Club
5580 Centerview Drive
Suite 200
Raleigh, NC 27606

919-233-9767

United Kennel Club
100 East Kilgore Road
Kalamazoo, MI 49001-5598
616-343-9020

Mixed Breed Dog Club of America
13884 State Rt 104
Lucasville, OH 45648-8586
614-259-3941

United States Border Collie Handlers' Association, Inc.
Route 14A
Crawford, TX 76638

Australian Shepherd Club of America
6091 E. Hwy 21
Bryan, TX 77803-9652
409-778-1082

North American Hunting Retriever Association
P.O. Box 1590
Stafford, VA 22555
800-421-4026
703-221-4911

Tracking Tests

Tracking Tests demonstrate a dog's ability to follow a scent trail. For more information, please contact these clubs.

American Kennel Club
5580 Centerview Drive
Suite 200
Raleigh, NC 27606
919-233-9767

United Kennel Club
100 East Kilgore Road

Kalamazoo, MI 49001-5598
616-343-9020

Mixed Breed Dog Club of America
13884 State Rt 104
Lucasville, OH 45648-8586
614-259-3941

Flyball

Flyball is team sport made up of four dogs per team. It is a
competitive relay race. Each dog is required to jump four
hurdles and retrieve a tennis ball by stepping on a spring-
loaded box that shoots out the ball. The dog catches the ball
and returns to the start line. The next team member then starts
until all team members have finished. Two teams compete
against each other. The first team to finish without errors
wins. To find out more about Flyball, contact the following
groups.

North American Flyball Association
PO Box 8
Mount Hope, ON, LOR 10
Canada

Mixed Breed Dog Club of America
13884 State Rt 104
Lucasville, OH 45648-8586
614-259-3941

Frisbee

Alpo dog food, part of the Friskies PetCare Company,
sponsors the Canine Frisbee Disc Championships in commu-
nities throughout the U.S. Everyone is welcome to compete.
There are no entry fees and discs are provided.

Championships include Mini-Distance and Freeflight. Mini-
Distance is a timed event that is scored on a catch scale.

Points are awarded on the distance of the catch along with extra points for mid-air catches. Freeflight is a timed event that is scored on degree of difficulty, execution, leaping agility, and showmanship. Contact Friskies for more information.

Friskies Canine Frisbee Disc Championship
PO Box 725
Encino, CA 91426
800-423-3268

Friskies Canine Frisbee Disc Championship
4060-D Peachtree Rd #326
Atlanta, GA 30319
800-786-9240

Lure Coursing

This activity is designed for breeds that hunt by sight. The dogs chase a lure (simulated live game) over an open course. The lure is dragged across the ground at fast speeds in an irregular pattern much like a live game. Lure Coursing tests the dogs speed, ability to follow the lure, enthusiasm, endurance, and agility. For more information, contact the following groups.

American Sighthound Field Association
Newcomer Information Services
860-560-0533

American Kennel Club
5580 Centerview Drive, Suite 200
Raleigh, NC 27606
919-233-9767

Schutzhund

This German sport tests a dogs endurance, ability to scent, courage, mental stability, and trainability. It combines tracking, obedience, and protection exercises. Contact the USCA for more information.

USCA - United Schutzhund Clubs of America
3810 Pauli Avenue
St. Louis, MO 63125-1718
314-638-9686

Coonhound

Only Coonhounds participate in this sport. The dogs track
and tree raccoons. Once the raccoons are treed, the dog
signals the handler. To learn more about this sport, contact
the following clubs.

American Kennel Club
5580 Centerview Drive
Suite 200
Raleigh, NC 27606
919-233-9767

United Kennel Club
100 East Kilgore Road
Kalamazoo, MI 49001-5598
616-343-9020

Earthdog Tests

These tests for small terriers and Dachshunds are designed to
measure the dog's hunting and working abilities. According
to the AKC, "The noncompetitive program begins with a
basic introduction to den work and quarry and progresses
through gradual steps to require the dog to demonstrate that it
is capable of being trained to follow game to ground and work
its quarry." For more information, please contact the following group.

American Kennel Club
5580 Centerview Drive
Suite 200

Raleigh, NC 27606
919-233-9767

Cat Clubs

There are a number of cat registries for purebred and mixed breed cats that sponsor cat shows throughout the U.S.

American Cat Fanciers' Association
PO Box 203
Point Lookout, MO 65726
417-334-5430

Cat Fanciers' Association
1805 Atlantic Avenue
Manasquan, NJ 08736
908-528-9797

International Cat Association
PO Box 2684
Harlingen, TX 78551
210-428-8046

American Cat Association
8101 Katherine Ave
Panorama City, CA 91402
818-781-5656

Traditional Cat Association
18509 NE 279th St.
Battle Ground, WA 98604

Happy Household Pet Cat Club
260 Corral Ave.
Sunnyvale, CA 94086
408-732-2574

American Association of Cat Enthusiasts
P.O. Box 213
Pine Brook, NJ 07045
201-335-6717

Volunteer Opportunities

Non-profit groups are always in need of volunteers or donations. Volunteering can mean hands-on activities like walking dogs, playing with cats, picking up after them, petting them, and grooming. Other activities may include adoption counseling, event participation, education programs, and administrative help. Volunteer organizations can always use financial donations and most groups usually have a wish-list of needed items like leashes, chew toys, cat toys, etc.

Many groups allow children to participate. However, there may be a minimum age requirement. In addition, some groups have a minimum time commitment. For example, they may ask volunteers to commit to a six-month volunteer obligation.

NOTE: Check with your local animal welfare organizations, they are always in need of volunteers or donations.

If you are interested in donating your time or money, there are many non-profit groups that would love your participation. Call local humane societies, animal control, and other animal non-profit groups in your area and ask what programs are available. You're bound to find a group that fits your interests. Your help is genuinely appreciated no matter how big or small!

Chapter 4

Travel

Just because your little Tiffany has been hinting for a vacation doesn't necessarily mean she's well-suited for travel. In fact, most pets are creatures of habit and probably prefer the familiar surroundings of home to the exciting world of travel. For some pets, changing routines can be very upsetting, while other pets relish the chance to spend quality time with you exploring new places. Before taking your pet on a trip, consider the overall well-being of your pet. Does your pet enjoy rides in the car, how will she do with extended drive time? Will she be a participant in the vacation or will she be left behind bored, worried, or frightened in the hotel?

Before taking your pet, talk with your veterinarian to ensure your pet is ready for the rigors of travel. Age, temperament, and health are all factors to be considered.

Be sure your pet is welcome. Don't assume an invitation for

TIP:
Before taking your pet, talk to your veterinarian to ensure your pet is ready for the rigors of travel. Also confirm accomodations for your pet.

your family includes your pet. Even though you consider your pet part of the family, your hosts may not. Confirm accommodations for your pet.

Don't Take a Pet on a Trip if It is . . .

- very shy

- aggressive

- unmanageable

- sick

- prone to motion sickness

- a female and in heat

- not housebroken

- not obedience trained

- not good with strangers

Packing For Your Pet

Taking a pet on a trip requires some preparation. Here's a list of recommended items to include in your packing.

- pet bed

- favorite pet toys or chews

- pet ID tags and license

- room deodorizer (good for car and overnight stays)

- collar and regular leash, plus a long leash
- training collar
- any current medication(s) enough for the trip plus 2-3 day emergency supply
- towels
- cleaning supplies (accidents can happen anywhere)
- paper towels
- pet treats
- pet food, enough for the trip plus 2-3 emergency supply
- pet first-aid kit (2" bandages, antibiotic ointments, gauze, tape, hydrogen peroxide, alcohol, tweezers)
- food and water bowls
- plenty of water
- dog scoop
- cat Litter box and litter
- health certificate
- pre-moistened towelettes
- recent photo
- crate (if pet has been crate trained)
- soap or shampoo
- pet towel
- brush and flea comb
- flea, tick and other insect repellants
- dog pack
- pet sweater or parka, consider weather conditions
- sunscreen
- proof of vacinations, health records, or health certificate

- Canine Good Citizen certificate or obedience completion certificate

Airplane Travel

Unless you absolutely must transport your pet by air, avoid taking pets on airplanes. Carefully consider the necessity of the trip. Is this the only way to get your pet to your destination? Must he go on this trip? Pet parents are risking their pet's health, safety and even life when putting him on an airplane. Are these risks absolutely worth taking?

Pets That Should Not Fly

- Pug-nosed cats or dogs (Chow Chows, Persians, Pekinese, etc.). Because of their short nasal passages, these pets are vulnerable to oxygen deprivation and heat stroke while in the cargo area.
- Pets less than 8 weeks old

- Females in heat

- Sick or frail pets

- Pregnant pets

Talk to your veterinarian about your plans to travel. Does your veterinarian believe that your pet is in good health to fly? Should your pet have any medication to help reduce the stress? Or, would medication do more harm than good? Airlines will require a health certificate and documentation of rabies shots and vaccinations before flight.

TIP: Make airline reservations early, there is a limit to the number of pets per flight. And book direct flights to reduce stress on your pet.

Make your reservations with the airline early. There is a limit to the number of pets that can travel on each flight. Avoid traveling during busy times of the year such as holidays or spring break. Book direct flights to reduce stress on your pet and to avoid baggage handlers losing your pet during a connection. Your luggage won't mind a night in Beijing, but your St. Bernard would. Each minute in the airport is bound to be stressful for your pet. If the airline tries to reroute you or book you on a later flight ask questions and express your concerns. Knowing that you're traveling with a pet will help the airlines to better accommodate you and your pet's needs.

Consider climate when booking your flight. Cargo areas are not temperature controlled. Book evening flights in hot weather and day time flights in cold weather. For the safety of your pet, do not fly when it is either less than 40 degrees or more than 80 degrees in either the city you are departing from or arriving in.

Before boarding the plane, ask the flight attendant to remind the captain that your pet is aboard. Confirm that he has boarded. And by all means, report mishandling of any pets by airline employees.

Airline Approved Pet Carriers

Airlines will require that your pet travel in an approved crate or pet carrier. Attach a "Live Pet" tag that contains your name, address, telephone number, and flight information. Some people include a note such as:

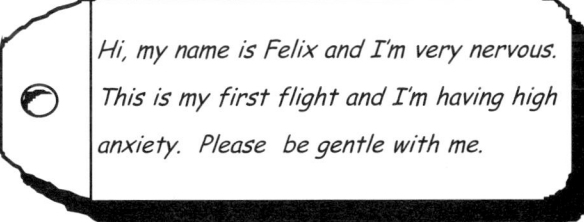

Hi, my name is Felix and I'm very nervous. This is my first flight and I'm having high anxiety. Please be gentle with me.

This is a nice reminder to airline personnel to take extra care of your beloved pet.

Be sure the latch is secured, but not locked. In the case of an emergency, airline personnel may need to release pets. If your pet carrier fits under your seat, your pet can travel in the main cabin with you.

Layer the bottom of the carrier with newspaper to insulate and absorb moisture. For your pet's peace of mind add a towel, blanket, or an old piece of your clothing to remind him of you. Food and water bowls should be secured in a crate or attached to the outside of the crate. Do not leave food in the crate. Fill water bowl with a block of ice to avoid water spilling.

Before Departure

- Clip your pet's nails to ensure they do not hook onto the crate door or other objects.
- Pack a current photo of your pet in case he is lost in transit.
- Thoroughly exercise your pet before the flight.
- Do not feed your pet 12 hours prior to flight (water is fine until leaving).
- Before boarding, take your pet for a walk and encourage him to go to the bathroom.

Upon Arrival

You've made it! Immediately take your pet out of carrier and examine him for injury or distress. Take him to a veterinarian immediately if there are any problems. If all seems well, congratulate your travel hound, give him some water, and take him for a walk.

Car Travel

TIP: The safest place to keep your pet while traveling in the car is in the back seat and preferably in a crate. Cats prefer to be in their crates.

When taking pets on car trips, preparation can minimize stress and maximize comfort for your pet and you. Before you begin your trip, make sure your pet has identification tags on. Bring along his collar, leash, first aid kit, water and bowl, and waste bags. Remember to bring pet's current health records and recent photos. Encourage him to go to the bathroom before you leave. Plan on stopping every two-to-four hours for water, exercise, and bathroom breaks.

The safest place to keep your pet is in the back seat and preferably in a crate. Cats are more comfortable and safer in their carriers. There are also seat-belt harnesses available for dogs.

Be sensitive to the fact that the temperature in the back seat may be different than what you are experiencing in the front. Just because you're doing fine doesn't mean your pet is too.

While you want to get lots of fresh air circulating around the car, be cautious when allowing dogs to stick their heads out the window. He'll get a cool breeze, but he may also get hit by debris. An airborne pebble can be mighty painful if it hits your pet in the eyes, nose, mouth, or face. Cold air may also harm pet's lungs, so do not let him keep his head out the window for extended periods. For these reasons and other safety risks, do not use open flatbed trucks to transport pets.

Be sure pets have plenty of room to move around comfortably. Include your pet on rest stops so he gets a chance to get out of the car and move about. During these breaks, be sure to keep your pet on a leash. Avoid leaving your pet alone in the car. This invites pet theft and can be dangerous on warm or cold days.

Pack food in heavy-duty zip lock bags. Heavy duty plastic bags also work well for water bowls. Keep a water bowl with water or ice available to pet. When you park, find a shady spot so pets don't overheat in the car.

To avoid car sickness, allow one hour for pets to digest food. Be sensitive to signs of motion sickness. Drooling, restlessness, anxiety, vomiting, or looking distressed are all signs of potential trouble.

Even on cool days, the sun can heat up a car quickly. But on hot days, the risk of overheating your pet is even greater. The temperature inside a car can reach deadly temperatures in a matter of minutes, and that's with the windows partially opened! Overheating can cause brain damage and death. Never leave your pet in a car on a warm day, even with the windows cracked. Don't do it.

On cooler days, when you must leave your pet in the car, be sure to park in the shade. Leave the windows cracked, but not enough to allow someone to break in or to allow your pet to get caught. Set a bowl of cool water on the floor.

Check the EMERGENCY CARE section for treating heat stroke.

Hotel Stays

NOTE: Hotels expect your pet to be housetrained and well-behaved. Be courteous and pickup after your pet.

If your travels require an overnight stay, there are thousands of hotels in the United States that welcome pets. Hotels expect your pet to be housetrained and well-behaved. Basic courtesies will go a long way in keeping pets welcome at these hotels.

Be Kind to Pet-Friendly Hotels By . . .

- picking up after your pet
- acknowledging and paying for any damages
- feeding your pet on the bathroom floor
- setting pet's towel or blanket down on his sleeping area to prevent shedding on furniture, bed, or carpet
- confirming your pet's reservation along with yours

Be Kind to Your Pet By . . .

- bringing his favorite toys, blanket, or bed

- keeping him on a leash to minimize his chances of getting lost

- asking hotel about exercise areas for pets

- taking him with you, not leaving him in the hotel

- leaving information at the front desk about where you are going and when you'll be back (if you absolutely must leave pet alone)

- leaving the front desk with a telephone number and emergency instructions

- crating him if you must leave him alone

- leaving television on to mask noises that may frighten your pet or cause him to bark

National Lodging Contacts

There are thousands of hotels and motels throughout the U.S.A that are pet-friendly. When making your reservations, be sure to confirm that you will be bringing your pet.

The following is a list of national contact numbers of known pet-friendly accommodations in the United States. Pet policies vary by management and location. Be sure to confirm that your pet meets any weight restrictions. Many of the hotels and motels only allow pets weighing less than 25 pounds. Also, ask about any additional pet fees or deposits, some of which may not be refundable.

Best Western	800-528-1234
Clarion Inns	800-228-5150
Comfort Inns	800-228-5150
Days Inn	800-325-2525
Doubletree	800-528-0444
Econo Lodge	800-553-2666
Friendship Inns	800-453-4511
Hampton Inn	800-426-7866
Holiday Inns	800-465-4329

Howard Johnsons	800-654-2000
Marriott	800-228-9290
Motel 6	800-466-8356
Quality Inns	800-228-5151
Radisson Hotels	800-333-3333
Ramada Inns	800-272-6232
Residence Inns	800-331-3131
Rodeway	800-228-2000
Sheraton-The Luxury Collection	800-325-3589
Sleep Inns	800-627-5337
Summerfield Suites	800-833-4353
Super 8	800-843-1991
Travelodge	800-255-3050
Vagabond Inns	800-522-1555

If Pet is Lost During Travel

So, young Missy ventured out to do some sightseeing on her own. Problem is, now she can't find her way back to you. Organize a search party immediately. Time is critical so don't delay. If you haven't found her within a few hours, call every animal shelter and humane society within 60 miles and check with them daily. Post "Lost Pet" signs with photo or description of the pet at busy intersections, stores, and veterinary clinics. Enlist the help of local letter carriers and police officers. While they walk their route and beat, they can keep an eye opened for your pet. Place a "Lost Pet" ad in the local newspaper that includes your pet's description and how to contact you. A frightened and disoriented pet can take days or weeks to allow a stranger to approach him, so be persistent. It may take a while, but keep calling and searching.

See LOST & FOUND section for more information on what to do.

What to Do if You Can't Take Your Pet

There are a number of options to consider if you must leave your pet behind while you travel. You may be fortunate enough to have a reliable friend, family member, or neighbor who gladly cares for your pet while you're away. If not, then your options are to hire a pet-sitter or to drop your pet off at a boarding kennel.

NOTE: Given the right sitter, you can travel worry-free, knowing that your pets and home are being cared for. Your friends and family will appreciate this.

Pet-Sitters

Your friends and family will appreciate this option. By hiring the right sitter you can travel worry-free, knowing that your home and pet are being cared for.

Not only will a pet-sitter feed, water, exercise, medicate, and play with pets, but she will also take care of your home. This may include things like watering plants, bringing in mail, opening and closing drapes, and turning lights on and off. If your pet won't be traveling with you, it would probably be happier staying at home rather than at a kennel. Pet-sitters can either stop by a certain number of times per day or stay in your home for round-the-clock petcare. Pet-sitters can be a particularly good option if your pet is older or has health concerns. Pets can become depressed or anxious while the family is away. Daily visits from a sitter will comfort your pet. Just listen to what Gus Greyhound had to say about his recent pet-sitter:

"*Okay, so my parents are all like packing suitcases and humming Don Ho tunes so I know what this means — vacation time. Last time the furless ones went away, I went to a kennel. The staff was nice and all, but this cat kept sneezing and one of the puppies kept howling all night long. There was this totally cute whippet, but I hardly got a chance to bark with her. Anyway, I'm thinking, okay back to the kennel with me, but then my family just kisses me goodbye and leaves. Whoa! So I'm thinking right-on — party time! I give my super high-pitched howl so the whole neighborhood knows it's time to PARTY. But just as I'm breaking out the kibbles, I hear these keys opening the front door. It's that furless lady that was here with Mom yesterday, petting me and telling me what fun we were going to have. But I don't want her at my party. All the dogs will think I'm a total geek having a human chaperon. But wait, she brought in the mail and the newspaper and watered the plants. Cool! That's one less thing for me to do. Then she closed the drapes, filled my food bowl, and cleaned out the cat litter. (I can't believe they go in the house — gross!) After that, she gave me my medication — oops, I would have forgotten about that. She then took me for a nice long walk, played ball with me in the backyard, and petted me under the chin. Before she left, she then turned on some music. Could this be? Might it be? Could this be my very own party planner? Oh yes! How cool! I'm totally psyched for the raddest party ever. Yippee, I love my parents. This beats the kennel any day of the week."*

P.S. "She even played hide and seek with our cat!"

Gus was a little disappointed to discover that his sitter wasn't there to cater a party, but he soon discovered she could be useful in other ways. She kept the food coming, walked him regularly, and did little chores around the house. Overall, she kept him on his routine, and Gus was glad to have her around.

You can hire a professional pet-sitter or employ someone you already know to watch your pets while you're away. This will reduce the stress on your friends, not to mention any of your own worrying! Interview potential sitters to see how well she interacts with your pet. Does your pet seem to like the prospective sitter? Does the sitter seem affectionate, capable, and responsible?

Exercise the same care selecting a pet as you would in selecting a veterinarian for your pet. If you are having difficulty finding a pet sitter, you may contact the following group for referrals in your area.

Pet Sitters International
418 E. King St.
King, NC 27021
Referral Line 800-268-7487
910-983-9222

National Association of Pet Sitters
Locator Line 800-296-7387

Questions to Ask

- How long have they been in business?
- Are they licensed and bonded?
- What is their level of experience?
- How would they handle an emergency? Do they have a backup plan in case they have an emergency?
- Can they provide three references?

Things to Discuss

- Be sure sitter has specific instructions about feeding, medication, exercise, play, etc.
- Make sure they have a list of emergency telephone numbers, including your veterinarian, a neighbor, friend and a backup sitter in case something happens to her.
- Leave your itinerary and telephone numbers.

Boarding

Before you make your reservation to board your pet, tour the facilities to be sure it is a safe and caring environment. Does the facility look and smell clean? Do the cages and runs seem big enough to comfortably suit your pet's needs? Do the other pets seem happy and well cared for? Is there adequate protection from the elements? Is the facility well-lit?

The following group can provide a listing of member kennels in your area.

American Boarding Kennel Association
4575 Galley Road, #400A
Colorado Springs, CO 80915
719-591-1113

Questions to Ask

- Do they belong to the American Boarding Kennel Association?
- How many staff members are on site? What about during "closed' hours?
- How is the temperature controlled? (Do they have air-conditioning and heating?)
- How frequently are pet areas cleaned?
- How often are pets exercised or played with?
- Is there a shaded outdoor exercise area?
- How often are pets groomed?
- Are pets groomed on-site or do they take them to another facility? (When pets are transported, there is a greater risk for problems like escapes or injuries during transport.)
- Do they allow personal items such as toys, blankets, and beds?
- Can your pet be fed her regular food to avoid diarrhea?
- What types of safety precautions are there? Are there smoke detectors, sprinklers, fire alarms, and staff on site for security?

TIP: Take personal items when you drop off your pet at a boarding facility. A bed, blanket, or toys will give your pet a sense of security.

Aside from the kennel's policies and procedures, you'll want to become acquainted with the staff and their philosophy on pet care. A loving environment will lessen the trauma of being away from home. Staff at a good kennel will handle your pet with care and sensitivity. They'll be working at the facility because they love animals and want to help make your pet's stay happy and healthy, not because there were no jobs at Wonder Burger.

If you are able, take your pet to the kennel to introduce her to the staff and show her where she will be staying. If the staff seems excited about meeting your pet and shows genuine concern for her, the kennel will probably be a good experience for your pet. If the staff rolls their eyes and mutters that you should get a life, it's probably not the environment you want for your pet.

When you drop off your pet, take some personal items to remind her of home. Her bed, blanket, or toys will help give her a sense of security. An old tee-shirt or something that smells like you will also comfort her during her stay. Remember to bring her food and medications along with any special instructions for care. It's always a good idea to leave your itinerary and emergency telephone numbers in case the kennel staff needs to reach you. Be sure to call the kennel to see how your pet is doing.

After you pick your pet up from her stay at the kennel, observe her for unusual behavior. Does she seem more aggressive? Timid? Fearful? If abnormal behavior persists, check with your veterinarian.

The downside to boarding pets at a kennel is that they are at greater risk of contracting infectious disease. Additionally, confined quarters and new environments can cause anxiety and depression.

Emergency Care

This section deals with two types of emergencies. First, accidents that require immediate first-aid and secondly, natural disasters that require emergency responses. Although you are probably not in a crisis at this moment, please review this section so that you will be better prepared to face an emergency should it arise.

Accidents

Accidents happen unexpectedly and your veterinarian may not always be available at the time and place you need him. Please take the time to familiarize yourself with the following emergency first-aid procedures so you are prepared to provide immediate care. Knowledge of first-aid procedures may save the life of your pet in an emergency.

If possible, call your veterinarian or an emergency care facility to coach you over the phone. And always follow-up with professional medical care from your veterinarian. Even if your pet seems fine af- ter you've provided immediate care, he may have internal injuries. Pets can appear to be fully recovered, then worsen days later.

TIP: Take the time to familiarize yourself with emergency first-aid procedures so you are prepared to provide immediate care.

If your pet is injured, do not give him water or other liquids. In case of internal injury, this could make his condition worse rather than provide the relief you intended.

Pet First Aid

In an emergency, first aid is not a substitute for veterinary treatment. However, if you are unable to get your pet to a veterinarian, knowing basic first-aid could save your pet's life. Always seek veterinary care following first-aid attempts.

BITE WOUNDS
Treatment/Action
Approach the pet carefully to avoid getting bitten. Muzzle the animal. Clean the wound with large amounts of water. Wrap large open wounds to keep them clean. Apply pressure to profusely bleeding wounds. Bite wounds often become in- fected and need professional care.
Call veterinarian.

BLEEDING
Treatment/Action
Apply firm, direct pressure over the bleeding area until the bleeding stops. Avoid bandages that cut off circulation.
Call veterinarian immediately.

BREATHING (pet stops breathing)
Treatment/Action

Check to see if the animal is choking on a foreign object (see Choking). If an object is removed from the throat and the animal still is not breathing, place the animal with its right side down. Close the animal's mouth and exhale directly into the nose, not mouth, until the chest expands. Cover the nose with a handkerchief or a thin cloth if preferred. Exhale 12 to 15 times per minute. At the same time apply heart massage with the other hand. The heart is located in the lower half of the chest behind the elbow of the front left leg. Place hand over the heart and compress the chest 1 to 2 inches for large animals, 1 inch for small animals. Apply heart massage 70-90 times per minute.
Call veterinarian immediately.

BURNS (chemical, electrical and heat)
singed hair, blistering, swelling, redness of skin
Treatment/Action
Flush burn area immediately with large amounts of cold water. Apply ice pack for 15-20 minutes.
Call veterinarian immediately.

CHOKING
difficulty breathing, excessive pawing at mouth, blue lips and tongue.
Treatment/Action
Look into the mouth to see if foreign object in throat is visible. Clear the airway by removing the object with pliers or tweezers, being careful not to push it farther down the throat. If the object remains lodged, place your hands on both sides of the animal's rib cage and apply firm, quick pressure. Or place the animal on its side and strike the side of the rib cage firmly with the palm of your hand 3 or 4 times. Repeat this procedure until the object is dislodged.
Call veterinarian immediately.
(see breathing)

DIARRHEA
Treatment/Action
Withhold food for 12-24 hours. Give ice cubes only.
Call veterinarian.

FOREIGN OBJECTS IMBEDDED
Porcupine quills
Sharp , hollow shafts.
Treatment/Action
Quill cannot be pulled out without anesthesia.
Call veterinarian.

Foxtails
A barbed seed sometimes visible in eye, nose,
mouth, throat or skin causing severe irritation.
Treatment/Action
Foxtails are usually too deep to remove without general anesthetic.
Call veterinarian.

FRACTURES
pain, inability to use leg
Treatment/Action
Muzzle animal and control bleeding. Watch for any signs of
shock. DO NOT TRY TO RESET A FRACTURE. Transport the animal to the veterinarian immediately using a
stretcher.
Call veterinarian immediately.

HEAT STROKE
rapid or difficulty breathing, vomiting, high body
temperature, collapse
Treatment/Action
Place animal in a tub of cold water, gently soak with a garden
hose or wrap in a cold, wet towel.
Call veterinarian immediately.

INSECT BITES
onset of swelling, itching and pain within one hour of bite.

Treatment/Action
Remove stinger and apply cold packs. If isolated from veterinary care, a topical cortisone or an anti-inflammatory ointment can be rubbed on area of bite. A previously prescribed antihistamine may be give orally.

Call veterinarian.

POISONING
vomiting, convulsions, diarrhea, salivation, weakness, depression, pain

Treatment/Action
Write down what the pet ingested and how much. Immediately call the veterinarian or poison control center. Do not induce vomiting or attempt treatment without direction from the doctor. In the case of poisoning on the fur or skin from oils, paints or chemicals, wash the animal with mild soap and rinse well.

Call veterinarian.

National Animal Poison Control Center

- Emergency Number 800-548-2423
  $30 charge, major credit cards accepted

- Non-Emergency Number 900-680-0000
  $20 minimum charge for 1st five minutes, $2.95 for each additional minute, $30 maximum charge

SEIZURES
salivation, loss of control of urine or stool, violent muscle twitching, loss of consciousness.

Treatment/Action
Move pet away from any objects that could be dangerous. Use a blanket for padding and protection. Do not put yourself at risk by restraining the animal during the seizure. Time the seizure, it usually lasts only 2 or 3 minutes. Afterwards, keep the animal calm, quiet, and cool.

Call veterinarian immediately.

SHOCK
irregular breathing, dilated pupils
Treatment/Action
May occur with serious injury or fright. Keep animal gently restrained, quiet, and warm with head elevated.
Call veterinarian immediately.

SNAKEBITE (poisonous and nonpoisonous)
rapid swelling, skin puncture, pain, weakness, shock
Treatment/Action
Stop all exercise to prevent spread of venom. Clean area. Many poisons damage nerves or body tissue on contact.
Call veterinarian immediately.

VOMITING
Treatment/Action
Withhold food for 12-24 hours. Give ice cubes for two hours after vomiting stops. Then slowly increase the amount of water and foods given over a 24-hour period.
Call veterinarian.

EMERGENCY EQUIPMENT
Muzzle
Use a strip of soft cloth, rope, necktie or nylon stocking. Wrap around the nose, under the chin and tie behind the ears. Care must be taken when handling weak or injured animals. Even normally docile pets will bite when in pain. Allow animal to pant after handling by loosening or removing the muzzle. Do not use a muzzle in a case of vomiting. Cats and small pets may be difficult to muzzle. A towel placed around the head will help control small pets making sure the pet can breathe.

Stretcher
A door, board, blanket or floor mat can be used as a stretcher to transport injured or weak animals.

Pet First Aid reprinted with the permission of the AAHA - American Animal Hospital Association.

Natural Disasters

Since you to cannot prevent natural disasters, the next best thing to do is prepare for them. This means having an emergency plan along with necessary supplies for possible disasters such as hurricanes, fires, earthquakes, or tornados.

Disasters are frightening for pets. Like humans, pets should be checked for injuries and signs of shock. If your pet is in shock after an emergency, he may pant heavily, pace, behave frantically, or have chills. If you suspect your pet is in shock, wrap him in a blanket or towel, keep him calm, and try to soothe him with reassurance. Call your veterinarian immediately.

Emergency Supplies

Keep supplies together in a sealed waterproof container that will be easily accessible in an emergency. An old duffel bag or backpack will fare well against the elements.

✓ activated charcoal tablets

✓ can-opener if needed for food or supplies

✓ carriers/crates for pets

✓ collar and leash

✓ copies of health certificate, license, and vaccination

✓ cotton balls and swabs

✓ diarrhea medicine

✓ emergency phone numbers (veterinarian, pet care)

✓ flame retardant blankets

✓ flea products

✓ food and water bowls

✓ food and water (two-week supply)

✓ litter and pan

✓ medication (two-week supply)

✓ pet first-aid kit (2" bandages, antibiotic ointments,gauze, tape, hydrogen peroxide, alcohol, tweezers)

✓ petroleum jelly

✓ plastic bags for waste

✓ recent photos

✓ rectal thermometer

✓ scissors

Emergency Drills

Decide in advance who does what in an emergency. Which family member will gather pets and supplies? Have regular emergency drills to keep the plan fresh in the minds of your family members. Post emergency stickers on your front door or window to notify fire fighters that pets are inside. Fire fighters will make every attempt to save your pet.

Emergency Information

Keep an emergency care information card in your wallet and posted on your refrigerator. On the card, list the telephone numbers and addresses of your veterinarian and people who will temporarily house your pet in an emergency. Provide all relevant information about your pets in case you are unable to care for them after an emergency.

For your wallet

EMERGENCY CARE FORM

In Case of Emergency Notify:

(Name) _____(Phone) _____

Pet Name(s) _____

Veterinarian Name _____(Phone) _____

Veterinarian Address _____

Owner's Name _____

Owner's Phone(s) _____

Additional Contacts _____

Special Needs _____

For your refrigerator

EMERGENCY CARE FORM

In Case of Emergency Notify:

(Name) _____(Phone) _____

Pet Name(s) _____

Veterinarian Name _____(Phone) _____

Veterinarian Address _____

Owner's Name _____

Owner's Phone(s) _____

Additional Contacts _____

Special Needs _____

Lost & Found Pets

Aside from a trip to the veterinarian, nothing is more frightening for a pet than being lost. All that's familiar to your pet is suddenly gone and has been replaced with the unknown.

Simple precautions can help find a lost pet, or better yet, prevent the problem all together. Make sure all pets have identification tags that include your home telephone number. Have a clear color photo of your pet on hand to help others identify him.

Train your pet not to dart out the door, and never leave your pet unattended in a parking lot or outside of a store.

Check Inside the House

If your pet turns up missing despite these precautionary measures, the first place to search is around the house. Think about places you might have accidentally trapped your pet like the attic, basement, closet, or cabinets.

Dangerous Liaisons

Check the refrigerator right away. Your pet isn't likely to be there, but in the rare event she is, your chilly dog or cold kitty will greatly appreciate a quick escape to room temperature. If your washer and dryer are running, check them immediately. The spin cycle is no place for a land-loving pet.

Other Places in the House

Pets are curious little critters and want to explore areas of the house. Think about all the places small enough to fit your pet. Could kitty have filed himself in your file cabinet? Could he be immersed in a great novel behind the bookshelf? Perhaps he's tucked away in your Lazy Boy? Small pets love to explore the world of box springs and bedding. Kitty may be a Santa Claus impersonator and be hiding in the fireplace. (If you find him there, remember to wash paws thoroughly to avoid a house full of cinderprints.) You may find your pet in a suitcase. (If he's wearing your Hawaiian shorts, your clever kitty is telling you he needs a vacation.) How about in or behind an appliance? If kitty shows talent for vacuuming and the like, you may want to consider cultivating these fine skills.

Your Search Outside

If you are still unable to find your pet, organize a search party immediately both by car and by foot. Call your pet by name and listen carefully. Leave his favorite person's laundry on the doorstep and walk barefoot so the pet can track the scent home. Ask neighbors, mail carriers, and garbage collectors if they have seen your pet. Copy a photograph of your pet to post with a "Lost Pet" sign. On your sign, include a photo, the pet's name and breed, and a telephone number to call for people to reach you. Offering a reward will greatly enhance your chances of recovering your pet. Distribute these fliers within a two-to-three mile radius from home, at local veterinary offices, animal shelters, pet stores, neighbors' homes, and on telephone poles.

Go to local animal shelters to see if anyone has found your pet, don't rely on anyone else to identify your pet for you. Place a lost ad in the local newspaper. Check the found ads. Many papers offer this service for free.

Finally, don't give up. It could take weeks or even months to find your lost pet. He's trying to find you just as hard as you are trying to find him. Usually, it's just a matter of time before you reconnect with your wayward pet.

TIP:
Leave his favorite person's laundry on the doorstep and walk barefoot so your pet can track the scent home.
DON'T GIVE UP!

Found Pets

If you find a pet, approach him calmly and cautiously. Be sensitive to the fact that the pet is already frightened and will be alarmed by sudden moves. Check for identification tags. If there are tags, then contact the owner immediately. If there are no tags, have the pet checked for a microchip ID.

If the pet is injured, call animal control for assistance or take him to your veterinarian.

You then have two choices:

Choice One
Call or take him directly to the local animal shelter. This will probably be the first place an owner will check. You may consider checking on the pet in a few days to see if he's been claimed. If the pet is scheduled to be destroyed, you could perform a mission of mercy and help him get adopted. Perhaps this is the fates telling you it's time for another pet in your life.

Choice Two
Decide to keep the animal at your home and perform the nec-

essary steps in finding the owners. Remember, you are then responsible for the pet and its safety. Be careful.

The first thing to do is call the local animal shelters to find out if anyone is looking for the pet. The owner will likely call here first as well. Contact lost and found services, check lost ads in the newspaper, and talk to your neighbors. You should also place a found ad in the local paper.

Meanwhile, take a photograph of the pet and post "Found Pet" notices around town. While you're out, be on the look-out for "Lost Pet" signs. If you site a station wagon full of kids sobbing, "Lassie, come home," your days of surrogate pooch parenthood are probably over. On the other hand, if someone shows up claiming to be the owner, be sure to check for proof. A photo or veterinarian bill will suffice. If the person is unable to provide this information and the pet doesn't seem to recognize him, do not give him the pet. If he is truly the owner, he will appreciate your concern and return with the necessary information.

Chapter 7

Weather Tips

It is critical to be aware of how weather affects a pet's health and well-being. A pet left out on a very cold day can be struck by hypothermia or frostbite. On a hot day, a pet could suffer from heat stroke. Both can be life-threatening conditions.

Stormy Weather

Storms are scary. The roar of the thunder, the illuminated sky, it's straight out of a horror flick. There are a few things that can be done to help calm a pet during storms. Draw curtains or close blinds to hide lightning. Drown out the noise of thunder with music, an air-conditioner, or a television.

Cold Weather

Pets should be introduced to cold weather for short intervals at a time. Allow them to gradually get used to it before sending them out to trek the frigid tundra. Don't ever leave pets outside without shelter for extended periods of time in cold weather. This, along with leaving a pet in the car, can lead to hypothermia. If pets are wet or damp, do not let them out until they are dry. If the wind chill drops below 20 degrees, keep short-haired or small pets inside the house. Remember the less body weight and hair a pet has, the less protection he has against the elements.

When pets are going to be outside for a while, make sure they have fresh water (not ice) and an enclosed shelter to protect them from wind, snow, and rain. A shelter is most beneficial to your pet when it is elevated from the ground so moisture does not gather. A door or cover goes a long way in blocking out the elements and keeping your pet warm. Furnish the outdoor shelter with things your pet can snuggle into such as blankets, towels, warming pads, pillows, or even hay.

NOTE: The less body weight and hair a pet has, the less protection he has against the elements.

If the weather is harsh, bring pets inside the house. If your pet has been exposed to salt on the streets or sidewalks, rinse and dry their paws right away. Feed them more than you would normally because they need more energy and will be burning it quicker. Instead of bathing your pet in water, dry clean him (no, we don't mean send him to the cleaners!). Simply powder his fur with baby powder or corn starch and brush out thoroughly.

When you get into your car each morning, knock on the hood a few times or honk the horn to alert animals who may be making their winter home in your engine. Be aware that antifreeze is deadly to animals. If you spill antifreeze, clean it up right away so your pet or the neighborhood animals do not ingest it.

Hot Weather

The keys to preventing overheating are access to shade and water. Bring your pets inside on those sweltering days. As you step outside, ask yourself how you'd feel in a fur coat today.

If you take your pet in the car with you, be aware of the temperature in the back seat. You may be comfortable with the air-conditioner aimed at you, but how hot is your pet in the back of your vehicle? Park in the shade and keep all the windows cracked. They should be open enough to allow fresh air in, but not so much that pet can get stuck trying to escape. Of course, windows open too wide can lead to a break-in resulting in a stolen pet or car. Set a bowl of water on the floor for your pet to drink while you're away. Remember that even on mild days, the sun can warm a closed car quickly. On a hot day, a closed car can reach deadly temperatures in minutes which can kill a pet. For this reason, NEVER leave your pet in a closed car on a hot day!

TIP:
Never leave your pet in a closed car on a hot day, within minutes the car can reach deadly temperatures.

Be aware that a pet's fur acts as an insulator to heat as well as cold. Shaving your pets fur may sound like a good idea but could leave him vulnerable to the direct attack of the sun on his skin, as well as prevent him from cooling down.

Prevent burned pads by avoiding overheated surfaces, Protect your pet's nose and ears with sunscreen, they sunburn too. Use only pet-approved topical tanning lotions.

In addition to lots of water, give your pet ice cubes to munch on.

See the EMERGENCY CARE section on what to do if your pet is suffering from heat stroke.

Chapter 8

Photographing Your Pet

The keys to a successful photo session with your pet are patience, praise, and a sense of humor. Have fun and enjoy the photo session. Your pet will appreciate your sense of humor.

Before the photo session, give your pet a good brushing. Clean your pet's eyes and ears so that he'll look his very best for the camera. Begin by recruiting someone to help. The assistant's job is to help get your pet into the proper poses and keep him there. This is much easier said than done. Remember patience. This is not the time to upset your pet or for you to get stressed.

- Be ready to shoot quickly when the pose is struck.

- Keep the session short.

- If your pet is the primary subject, he should fill at least half the frame.

- Select a background that compliments your pet. Do not use a busy background that overwhelms your pet. A backdrop can be created by draping or hanging a towel or sheet behind your pet on a door, sofa, or wall.

- Shoot at pet's level. This may mean getting down on hands and knees. Or, a small pet could be elevated by placing on a chair or table.

- To reduce red eyes, avoid shooting your pet looking directly at camera. Try shooting pet at an angle. Avoid using a flash.

- When shooting outside, avoid bright sun and shoot instead in bright shade. The objective is to avoid dark shadows on pet. Position the pet so that the light hits him on the side, this will flatter his fur and face.

- Add bandanas or other props that might add interest or character to the photo. But be careful not to overdo it, the pet should remain the focal point.

- Use pet's favorite toy or treats to get his attention.

- Be sure to use the correct film for the lighting conditions at the photo site. For indoor photos use a higher ASA(200-400) unless you are using professional flashes. And, for outdoor photos use a lower ASA(100-200) depending on sunny or cloudy conditions.

- *Say "Pet Treat"!*

TIPS:
Shoot quickly when the pose is struck.
Select a background that compliments your pet. Shoot at your pet's level.

Chapter 9

Choosing a New Pet

So, you're thinking about getting a new pet. And why not? They're wonderful companions, love you unconditionally, and are as cute as can be. Like any relationship though, one should carefully consider this long-term commitment and closely examine your reasons for wanting a pet. Are you ready to assume responsibility for a pet for the next 10 to 20 years, or, have you thought that far ahead? Are you ready for the challenges of pet parenthood, or have you just thought about the fun stuff? Do you see your pooch as an addition to the family, or no more than a live alarm system?

Are You Ready For A Pet?

As a perspective pet parent, there are many things to consider before bringing a new pet home.

Time

Does your family's lifestyle leave room for daily walks, play, and care? Will you have time to make sure your pet keeps all veterinary appointments?

Cost

NOTE: Consider the long-term commitment (10-20 years) and closely examine your reasons for wanting a pet.

Can you afford the substantial cost to care for your pet? Food, toys, pet supplies, grooming, health, and dental care can add up quickly. If you're considering a large dog, realize that caring for a large dog is significantly more expensive than a smaller pet. Because of size and quantity, food, medication, pet supplies, and toys are more expensive for a large dog. You can expect to spend at least $400 a year for a cat and, depending on the dog, it could range from $500 to over $1,200 a year. In addition, there will be unexpected medical expenses. If you travel, there will be pet-sitting or boarding expenses.

Space

Do you have the space in your home to accommodate a pet? Where will your new pet sleep? Most pets prefer to sleep with you. Is there room in your bedroom for his bed? Where's the doggie diner? How about the kitty cafe? Small pets may be comfortable in a small apartment. However, most big dogs will require larger spaces to play, sleep, and exercise. Where will the pet bathroom(s) be located? Do you have a yard for pets to spend a little leisure time? How close are you to a park? Where will you exercise your pet?

Indoor/Outdoor

Will your pet be an indoor pet, outdoor pet, or have indoor and outdoor access? Some new dog owners believe dogs belong only in the backyard, but this rarely, if ever, works out well. A bored dog will soon look for ways to pass the time. Building a new deck and planting marigolds are not the constructive ideas they come up with. They usually occupy time with barking, chewing, digging, and escaping. Because they haven't gotten the attention needed, many backyard pets end up at the animal shelters. If you intend on keeping your dog outside, please consider a buddy for your pet. An outdoor pet will not require walks to relieve himself, however, he will still require daily attention, exercise, and playtime with you. Dogs are pack animals and are happiest in the company of others. Solitary confinement is a horrible sentence for them.

NOTE:
Because of all the potential dangers outdoors like cars, dogs, wildlife, and diseases, an outdoor cat has a much shorter expected lifespan.

For kitty's sake, if possible, keep him safe by keeping him indoors. Because of all the potential dangers outdoors like cars, dogs, wildlife, other cats, and diseases, an outdoor cat has a much shorter expected lifespan. Many cat owners have found ways to bring the excitement and adventure of the outdoors inside. Kitty can now stalk a mechanical mouse or chase a feather toy with the same vigor as she would the real thing. Placing bird feeders in strategic window locations can also add hours of entertainment for kitty.

Landlord Approval

Remember that episode of "I Love Lucy' when the Ricardos had to hide their puppy from Fred Mertz because no pets were allowed in the building? In the end, the pooch was discovered, but Fred changed his policy because little Ricky named the dog after him. Well, that was television. In real life, you and Fred Mutts would be outta luck. Get approval from your landlord first.

Family Members

How do other members of your family feel about a new pet?
Are they willing to pitch in to help care for the pet? Is anyone
allergic to pet hair or dander? Will other pets accept the newcomer?

Patience/Supervision

Bringing home a new pet is similar to bringing home a two
year old that will require constant supervision until it understands the house rules. Do you have the patience to make it
through the adjustment and training period which, depending
on the pet, could be months, maybe years? This may even
require professional help from obedience trainers, behavior
specialists, or veterinarians.

Responsibility - Whose will it really be?

In the majority of households, it's mom who's left holding the
doggie bag. Your kids will be convincing when they promise
they will be the pet's primary care givers. They're not lying,
they honestly believe what they're telling you. Don't you,
though. You're the grown-up. Separate fact from fiction and
realize that the kids will throw bones, play catch, and pet the
animals. You will disinfect urine stains, rid fleas, and vacuum
endless hair. How tolerant will you be of this additional
work?

What Kind of Pet?

Okay, you've reviewed the rewards and challenges of pet parenthood and have decided to go ahead and adopt a cat or dog.
Congratulations! Pet parenthood has its responsibilities, but it
can also be an endless source of joy.

But wait, you've still got a few more items to consider before
picking out a name and food dish. Cat or dog? Male or female? Big or small? Active or mellow? Consider the following.

Cat or Dog

There's the obvious size difference between cats and dogs. With the exception of toy dog breeds, cats are usually smaller. While dogs want to be your constant companion, cats tend to be more independent. Dogs require daily attention to walk, feed, exercise, and play. In contrast, cats can tolerate being left alone for longer periods of time and don't require walks. On the other hand, dogs think you're the greatest thing since sliced beef, while cats secretly think you're the servant who brings the sliced beef.

The Gender Thing

There is no personality difference between male and female pets who have been spayed or neutered. Females tend to be smaller than males. Whichever sex you decide on, plan to have your pet "fixed." Unneutered males will fight, spray, and experience frustration, while unspayed females are messy and will yowl an incessant mating call while in heat bringing (spraying) males right to your door.

Size

Cats tend to be relatively close in size. But, there are always those few that exceed standards. Size becomes a much bigger issue for dogs. So, if you're thinking about getting a dog consider what size dog suits your family's lifestyle? Do you have a big yard and a station wagon? Or, are you in a studio apartment in the city? If you have small children, consider that a larger dog could accidentally hurt your child. Equally possible is that your child could accidentally injure a small pet. On the other hand, we've seen plenty of big dogs who play gently with children and hysterical toy breed dogs we wouldn't leave alone with a donut, let alone our children. What size dog can you control? If you're considering a puppy that will be large when full grown, will you and other family members have the strength to control him? Also, keep in mind there is a direct correlation between the size of a dog and the size of potential problems. Where a small dog may chew a furniture leg, a large dog may destructively chew an entire sofa in an afternoon.

Dominant vs. Submissive

Think about the kind of people you like to hang out with. Are they big personalities or a little mellow? You'll probably want a pet who's a lot like your buddies. And what type of pet would be happiest in your home? Would your busy household be a frightening place for the shy submissive? Do you have the energy to keep up with your bold and curious little dominant?

Hair type

We don't mean put your dog's hair in a sweet little ribbon. In fact, please don't. It looks silly and other dogs will tease little Bergdorf. But do consider climate, grooming, and shedding in your decision whether to choose a long or short-hair pet. If you're not into high maintenance, then consider a short-hair pet.

Energy Level

Do you want a pet who's energetic and playful? Or gentle and calm? Some breeds are known for certain temperaments. The age of your pet will also be a factor in whether your pet wants to play ball or just watch a ballgame on TV with you.

Number of Pets

Consider two pets. Now, Noah also subscribed to the two pet theory, but for very different reasons. Since your spayed and neutered pets won't be reproducing anyway, we suggest two pets because they'll keep each other company. Coupled pets are happier and tend to be less destructive than a pet left home alone.

Age

For many reasons, we highly recommend considering an adult adoption. The most compelling reason is that adult pets are less likely to be adopted so you would be saving a pet. Adults are less expensive (they've already gone through all the baby

vaccinations and teething stage). What you see is what you get
- size, personality, and appearance. Many times they are already house-trained and may have some obedience
training. They're less fragile and
more mature, a perfect combination for a household with young
children. Patience and under-
standing will insure family bond-
ing. You may have to work with
some old habits, but teaching an
older dog new tricks is easier than
rumored.

Benefits of adult
pet adoptions:
1. Saving a pet.
2. Adults are less
   expensive.
3. Many are already
   house-trained.
4. They may have
   obedience training.

Perhaps you have your heart set on a puppy or kitten. It's hard
not to fall in love with those adorable sweet little bundles of
energy. Raising a young pet allows owners to play an active
role in shaping the pet's behavior. Pet "childhood" is a whirl-
wind of activity. They require constant supervision as they
chew, scratch, whine, bite, and investigate everything through
childhood. They've got a lot to learn and will need you to
teach them. Right now, they're cute little ones, sometimes
it's difficult to predict how their looks and personality will
develop. Pets should be at least eight weeks old before
going to a new home. They will need the first of many
veterinary visits to begin immediately.

Tips for Adopting a Pet

You may be asking yourself how in the world to figure all of
this out before adopting a pet. It's easy enough to ask the
breed, gender, and age. And it's easy enough to see the pet's
size and hair type. But how do you figure out if a pet's active,
submissive, independent, or sociable? Observe the pet for a
while. See how she acts with the others. Note whether she
seems friendly toward you or indifferent. When you approach
the pet, is she curious and eager to make friends? Or is she
shaking nervously, curled up in a ball under furniture? Be
aware of clues pets give you regarding who they are and what
they'll be like at home. However, if you're planning on adopting from a shelter, realize that the pet is in a stressful environ-

ment and will most likely not be himself. Once at home, you will probably see a new confident, relaxed, happy pet develop.

Where to Find a Pet

Because of the overpopulation of pets, there is an abundance of pets looking for good homes. Wonderful pets in need of homes can be found at local animal shelters and breed rescue groups.

Animal Shelters

Many special pets are waiting for homes at local animal shelters. Adopting a pet from an animal shelter not only saves a pet from possible death, but also makes room for another needy pet. Thousands of pets are abandoned each year because of negligence on an owner's part to care for and train their pet. When observing dogs at the animal shelter, remember that they are stressed, frightened, and lonely in this environment. Be patient and spend time with them to determine if they are the right one for you. Pets from the shelters will require sensitivity, love, and a lot of attention to help them with the transition. All pets adopted from shelters will have already been spayed or neutered.

Breed Rescue Groups

These groups are devoted to the well-being of specific breeds. Each year, thousands of purebreds are abandoned or turned in to shelters by their owners. Unlike human athletes, retired racing dogs do not look forward to lucrative product endorsements or careers in sports-casting. Instead, a greyhound might spend his retirement years with your family, regaling you with stories of his golden years on the track. A rescue group exists for almost every breed of dog. Similar to animal shelters, pets adopted through breed rescue groups will already have been spayed or neutered.

If you are interested in adopting a specific breed, ask your local veterinarian, animal shelter, breeder or dog show sponsor where to find that rescue group. Many breed rescue groups can be found listed on the World Wide Web. Or you may contact the following organization to find specific breed rescue groups nearest you.

Project BREED
P.O. Box 15888
Chevy Chase, MD 20825-5888
202-244-0065

Questions to Ask About an Adoptive Pet

Many people handling the adoption of pets will not have all the answers to your questions, or the information they have may be inaccurate. Nonetheless, it's a good idea to ask anyway.

1. Does the pet get along with others: children, men, women, other cats or dogs?

2. Is the pet house trained or obedience trained?

3. What kind of temperament does the pet have? Is it fearful or aggressive?

4. Does the pet need special care?

5. Does this pet or its breed have certain health or medical needs?

When pets are abandoned, their former owners usually did not take the time and give the attention needed, or they may be the victim of circumstance. Her owner may have died, divorced, moved, or had a baby. Perhaps a new landlord does not allow pets. Abandoned pets will need extra patience, attention, and training. Pets are not themselves at the shelters. Take them outside and give them a chance to calm down and get to know you. As she spends more time with you in a quieter, relaxed environment, you will see her confidence grow and personality shine through.

New Pet Care

Bringing home a new pet will require some preparation. Planning ahead will help insure a smooth transition for you and your new pet. This chapter will help you plan for those first few weeks with your new pet.

Prior to picking up your new pet, make an appointment with your veterinarian for the pet's first visit. If you have other pets at home, you may want to see your veterinarian first before taking your pet home.

Pet Supplies

Be prepared! Before bringing your new pet home, plan a shopping trip to pick up necessary pet supplies.

- Premium Nutrition Pet Food
  Abrupt changes in pet food can cause stomach upset and
  diarrhea. To avoid this problem, gradually mix new pet
  food with the old pet food so your pet can slowly become
  accustomed to the new food.

- Nutritious Pet Treats
  These will come in handy for training.

- Food and Water Bowls
  Untippable, porcelain, or stainless steel are recommended.
  Placing a mat under the bowls may help contain stray
  kibbles and water puddles.

- Collar (Avoid using a choke collar for everyday use.)
  Two fingers should fit between the collar and neck. Be
  sure to check fit regularly as pet grows. For cats, look for
  a strangle-proof, breakaway, or elastic sectioned collar.
  Some collars can be personalized with your pet's name
  and phone number.

- Identification Tags
  If your pet should get lost or injured, an identification tag
  is his best bet for finding his way home. People who find
  your pet will return him to you instead of taking him to
  the animal shelter or keeping him as their new pet. If the
  pet is injured, a vet is more likely to treat a pet with tags.
  Unfortunately, tags on collars can be removed either
  purposely or by accident. To safeguard your pet, in
  addition to tags, you may also wish to have your pet
  tattooed or have a small identification microchip inserted.
  Your vet can inject the microchip between your pet's
  shoulder blades without any pain to the pet. But, before
  microchipping your pet, contact your local animal shelters
  to find out if they scan for microchips. If they do, ask
  which manufacturer's chips they scan.

- Carrier or Crate
  Be sure to get one that is sized correctly for your pet. It is
  important not to get one that is either too large or too
  small for your pet.

- Odor and Stain Removers
  Even with adult adoptions, you will have mistakes. So, the best plan is to have supplies on hand when the need arises.

- Safe Toys
  Toys serve as playthings, boredom eliminators, and provide "teething" comfort for young pets. There are many toys available for dogs and cats. Please consider safety when purchasing toys. Similar to buying toys for children, avoid toys with squeakers, foam, those that can be swallowed, or toys with strings that a pet can become entangled in.

- Repellent or Chew Stops
  These products will help you keep kitty from dining on your favorite plant or puppy from nibbling on your furnishings.

- Grooming Supplies (shampoo, combs, brushes)
  Talk with your veterinarian or groomer about the specific grooming supplies needed for your new pet.

- Washable, Durable Bed
  A comfortable bed for your pet will help you and your pet sleep better. Trust me, when he's up, you will be too.

- Emergency Rescue Stickers
  They should indicate the number, name, and type of pets for each entrance to your home.

- Litter and Litter Box (for cats)
  Ask the previous owner what type of box and litter the cat was using. Any changes to box or litter type should be done gradually. The goal is to gain cat's acceptance. Sudden changes may send him looking for another spot.

- Scratching Post (for cats)
  Look for a sturdy post that doesn't sway or won't easily tip over. It should be tall enough for your cat to fully stretch and scratch. Place the scratching post in the area that your cat will spend most of his time.

- Baby gates (for dogs)
  Baby gates are great for confining new dogs, preferably in areas with scrubable floors. From a dog's perspective, he will be happier behind a gate that he can see through rather than a door that shuts him off from you.

Pet-Proofing Your Home

Take the time to walk through your home and pet-proof any possible dangers. Much like bringing a child into your home, you will need to make provisions for your pet's safety. Get down on your hands and knees and look for poisons, small or sharp objects, and other possible dangers.

*NOTE:
Much like bringing a child home, you will need to make provisions for your pet's safety. Look for poisons, small or sharp objects, and other possible dangers.*

New pets will sniff, lick, chew, tug, push, and bat anything they come across. They will jump and crawl into anything that seems of interest. Some are even pretty good at using their paws to open doors and cabinets.

Please be vigilant in removing hazards. Here are some hazards to be aware of.

- All medications, poisons, cleaning products, and anything else that would be harmful if ingested, should be locked away from pet's access.
- Remove valuables or breakables.
- Remove tablecloths or your new pet may end up pulling it off for you.
- Make sure that trash cans are not accessible.
- Never leave plastic bags out, a curious pet can quickly find themselves entangled and might suffocate.
- Remove drapery cords, string, yarn, and thread from pet's reach. These are dangerous if swallowed or entangled.
- Keep windows and stairway doors closed to prevent possible falls.

- Keep an eye on reclining chairs, small pets can get caught in the inner mechanism.
- Never leave pet unattended in kitchen with hot stove-top surfaces.
- Check dryer before turning on, cats have been known to hop into dryers for a little cat nap.
- Check with your veterinarian or local nursery about safe indoor and outdoor plants. Many plants are harmful and some even fatal for pets.
- Protect pet from chewing on electrical cords. Move cords out of pet's reach, use repellents, or use protective coverings on cords to prevent electrical shock. Always supervise your pet in areas with electrical cords.

Outdoor areas need to be pet-proofed as well. Walk around the outside of your home and look for possible dangers.

- Remove any antifreeze drippings.
- Store any poisons, pesticides, and other deadly products out of pet's reach.
- If possible, remove or cover wires, ropes, or cords that pet may chew or become entangled in.
- Walk fence-line and look for any possible escape areas and repair immediately.
- Be sure your fence is tall enough to prevent an aerial escape.

What to Expect ... the Good, the Bad, & the Ugly

You've probably already thought about all the **Good** stuff that comes from a new pet. There's the unconditional love, companionship, entertainment, and their playful spirit. These are probably the reasons you've chosen a pet.

Expect some **Bad** as in bad behavior, which may include barking, biting, yowling, scratching, chewing, just to name a few examples. Now, to your pet, what we call bad behavior may be perfectly normal and acceptable cat or dog behavior. But, as his human companions, we may find their behavior totally unacceptable. You will need to show him what is good versus bad behavior. He will not know the difference until you take time to show him.

Don't forget about the **Ugly**. This is the term used to describe all those surprises your pet will leave you like urine, vomit, spills, or broken possessions. No pet owner escapes these surprises. Count on it, you too will be gifted with these types of surprises.

As a new puppy parent, expect some chewed-up stuff, house training errors, and lots of puppy energy. Your puppy will probably be eager to sniff, chew, run, and investigate everything. You'll also get a chance to hear his vocal skills with a repertoire of barks, yowls, and whining. Some pets initially may be shy or confused. This is normal. With time, patience, and consistency your pet will fully adapt to his new environment.

From Miss Kitty, you can expect a flurry of activity - jumping, climbing, tumbling, and scratching are part of her routine. She'll chase her tail, never realizing the futility of this pursuit. She'll decide that your telephone cord is her mortal enemy and do battle with this spiral monster daily. Dull moments are rare in a house with a new kitten. During those quiet times, Miss Kitty will be curled up on the sunny spot of the floor, dreaming of a trip to the all-you-can-eat sushi bar.

The following is a 10-point plan to help maximize the good and minimize the bad and ugly:

1. **Give lots of love** and attention to your new pet. Be patient with him and forgive his inevitable mistakes. Take the time to enjoy your pet's homecoming and help him adjust to his new home. It is time well spent.

2. **Spend time at home** with your new pet, allowing him the opportunity to get used to his new environment. Respect his need for peace and quiet and resist the urge to over-handle.

3. **Take him on a guided tour** of your home right away. Show him his bed or crate, food and water bowls, and

bathroom area.

4. **Ease pet's transition with the familiar**. This can be done by bringing a towel or blanket from pet's first home to his new place. Feed pet what he's used to eating, slowly mixing it with new food. For cats, use the same cat litter that it's used to.

5. **Confine pet to a room** with an adult present. It's better to catch house training errors before, instead of after, they happen. If possible, keep your pet in a room with washable floors. This room should have food and water bowls and access to the bathroom area. For kitty, this means having the litter box in the room. For puppy, this means a paper area or access to outdoors to relieve himself. It's best to keep new cats confined for a few weeks until they are fa miliar with their new environment. This way you won't lose your new friend, and she won't lose sight of those very necessary items like the litter box.

6. **Put new pet on a schedule**. This schedule should include time for meals, bathroom duties (for dogs), play, and sleep. While this may seem as rigid as pet boot camp, a routine will help your new pet adjust to its new home.

7. **Place bed or crate in the bedroom** of the person respon sible for pet care. This is necessary for puppies so that the responsible person can take an awakened puppy out in the middle of the night to go to the bathroom. Being close to people will help him adjust to his new home away from lit-termates. A hot water bottle and blanket might be comforting to a puppy. Your new cat may prefer to sleep on your bed. If you don't want her on your bed, then you will need to provide her with an alternative that is agreeable to her.

TIP: Setting up a routine will help your new pet adjust to its new home.

8. **Visit the veterinarian** to ensure your pet is healthy and vaccinated on time.

9. **Socialization is an important part** of a puppy or kitten's development. Provide lots of opportunities for your new

pet to meet others. Show him off, he'll love the attention and who can resist a puppy or kitten. Puppies should remain at home until about sixteen weeks of age, and they are done with their early vaccinations. After that, they should be ready to meet the world. By introducing your pet to new people and situations, you help to boost your pet's confidence. This is especially important for timid pets.

10. **Have fun with your new pet.** Let him know you think he's wonderful to spend time with. Make time every day to play. You and your pet will love it.

How to Crate Train Your Dog

Like humans, dogs want a special place that's all their own. Kids build tree houses, adults invest in real estate. Our four-legged furry friends are no different. Giving your puppy a crate helps him feel safe and secure. Crates can be used as a house-breaking aid, a safe place for your pet, or for car or airline travel.

1. Select a crate that is big enough for pet to stand up, turn around, and lay down stretched out on his side. For puppies, there are crates available that expand with a dog's growth.

2. To begin training, leave the crate door open and put treats inside to reward puppy for going in. Make this a comfortable retreat for pet by placing a blanket and chew toys inside. Encourage pet to explore his new crate. Allow him to come and go at his own pace.

3. Once he is familiar with his crate, shut the crate door for a few minutes. Gradually build up the time spent in the shut crate.

4. The crate can be used for nighttime sleeping, day-time rest periods, and times when pet can't be supervised. Limit the time your pet is confined to the crate. He shouldn't be confined for hours on end or for the rest of his life. The crate should be used as a training tool and resting place, not a prison. Be sensitive to bathroom breaks by limiting the amount of time spent in the crate. Allow at least an

hour break between crate shut-ins.

5. Once puppy is house trained, leave the crate door open. You'll find him choosing his crate as his resting spot when he's tired.

TIP:

Limit the time your pet is confined to the crate. It should be used as a training tool and resting place, not a prison.

Don't

- get a crate that's too big
- force puppy inside crate
- worry that puppy will use crate to relieve himself
- puppies have an instinctive desire to keep their crate's clean
- leave puppy in crate all day
- make the crate a punishing place, his crate should not be associated with fear or punishment.

Housetraining Your Puppy

Housetraining can be fun and rewarding for both you and puppy. Well . . . maybe that's stretching it, but it doesn't have to be a major trauma either. It will take discipline and commitment, but the effort is well worth it. You know the consequences, enough said.

Creating a Routine

Establish routines with your new puppy, like taking walks at the same time every day. Good times to schedule walks are first thing in the morning, after puppy's meals and naps, and last thing before sleep. Take puppy to a designated spot for relief. (This is known as the L'Plaza du Pupu, if you have a poodle.) While a set routine is optimal, watch for signs that puppy needs to go. Don't ignore telltale signs such as sniffing, whining, turning in circles, and going to the door. In canine, this clearly translates to "Hurry up, I've gotta go!"

Your puppy depends on you for scheduled walks. The following chart helps identify how often puppy should be walked.

Puppy Age	_Walk Puppy every..._
6 weeks	4 hours
8 weeks	5 hours
12 weeks	6 hours
5-6 months	8 hours

If puppy doesn't relieve himself in 10 minutes, bring him inside and try again later. Don't play with him until after he relieves himself.

Teach phrases like "hurry up" and praise him when he does. Reward puppy's success by lavishing him with praise. You may be tempted to let puppy find a private place to go to on his own, but during training, you should supervise and keep him on his leash.

When you are not at home to supervise, try to keep puppy on washable floors. Set-off an area with a baby gate and make sure puppy has a space of his own like a crate or bed.

Avoiding Mistakes

Let's face it, puppy mistakes are no fun to deal with. In fact, they stink. But remember, puppies don't have mistakes in the house out of anger or stupidity. They do so because they haven't been taught otherwise. Accidents are human error, not puppy spite. If you think your pooch is trying to tell you he doesn't like you by messing on your carpet, you're wrong.

If you catch puppy in the middle of a mistake, startle him with a loud noise and take him to his outdoor spot. Never correct or punish after the fact. And by all means, don't rub puppy's face in his mistake. It doesn't teach him anything except fear, and it's just plain mean. If you find a mistake, simply clean it up and go on with the day. It is too late to make a fuss. There are a number of products on the market designed to clean and neutralize odors. In a pinch, a mixture of water and vinegar solution can be used to neutralize the odor. Never use ammonia. It will act as a magnet for puppy to "mark" that spot again.

Be sure to give puppy a "last call" before bedtime. If you have a very young puppy, be sensitive to signs of restlessness. Your puppy may not be able to make it through the night without another trip to the puppy rest stop. If you hear him moving about, take him out. Remember this is not playtime.

NOTE:
Puppies don't have mistakes in the house out of anger or stupidity. They do so because they haven't been taught otherwise.

Take him outside and then right back to bed. Otherwise, he may decide it's fun to wake you up each night for a little late evening play. If you're a sound sleeper, then set your alarm for 4 or 5 hours and take puppy outside.

After puppy is 4-5 months old, he should be housetrained and making few mistakes. If problems persist, ask your veterinarian to check for bladder infection or any other medical problem.

Puppies are eager to please and make you happy. By reinforcing good behavior and patiently redirecting mistakes, both puppy and you can soon establish a routine that keeps both of you happy. Then, you can move on to something really fun like chasing balls.

Pet Health Signs

You vowed to love your pet in sickness and in health, but how do you tell the difference? The language barrier poses a challenge to communications with your pet, but you can tell if she's not feeling well by observing physical signs and her demeanor. If you see any signs of illness or unusual behavior, contact your veterinarian.

Signs of Sickness...

- Lifeless, runny eyes

- Runny or dry nose

- Dull or eneven coat with a lot of shedding, baldness, dandruff or matting

- Scratching

- Ears red, smelly or filled with black, waxy substance

- Listless, unsociable

- Soft, runny or bloody stool

- Thin but potbellied (may be worms)

- Limps

- Doesn't eat

- Cries in pain

- Scaly, scabby or red skin

Households with Kids

A family pet is great opportunity for children to learn nurturing skills. Take the time and show children how to handle and care for the pet. It is very important that the parent supervise their interaction for the safety of both the child and the pet.

If you've ever wondered what may go through the mind of a young puppy placed in a new home with children then this may be how it goes:

Diary of a Puppy in a New Home

Dear Diary,

Today we went to the park for a picnic and played this really neat game where someone throws a ball to me, I catch it in my mouth, slobber all over it, and bring it back to do it all over again.

I had a good time and am adjusting to my new life with the furless, dry-nosed, two-leggers quite well. I love the family's two children, but am having a little difficulty with the younger one, Lloyd.

When Mom and Dad sprung me from the animal shelter, they showed little David and Lloyd how to approach me, holding their hands extended so I could get a good sniff and speaking to me in a soft gentle voice. They showed both boys how to pet me, pick me up, put me down, and let me sit in their laps. I know they've been trained, so I just can't understand why four-year-old Lloyd is so rough while his eleven-year-old brother handles me just fine.

Frankly, I feel a bit distressed by the fact that Lloyd seems to treat me like a toy, not a living thing, much less a member of the family. He picks me up by the scruff of the neck, pulls on my tail, chases me, drops me on the ground, teases me, and sometimes even hits me. Furthermore, I'm getting a little cranky 'cause every time I try to take a nap around this place, Lloyd starts yanking at my ears. When I go to my food bowl, there's Lloyd, ready to make my life difficult.

I really love the kid, I just wish his older brother or parents would spend a little more time redirecting his behavior. David seems to have the routine down pat. He's gentle, loving, and kind. Most importantly, he lets me be. He's quite a kid. I even see him wash his hands after handling me to avoid contact with any possible parasites I may have. (I'm so embarrassed!!)

Momma-furless is going to bring home a new baby soon, and I've already been briefed as to how we're going to handle the homecoming (okay, I overheard it, so what?!). First, they're going to bring me a piece of baby's clothing so I can get a good whiff of the little tike. Then, they're going to put me on my leash and let me approach the little cutie, since I already know my obedience commands. I can hardly wait. I've always wanted a pet baby!

I think I smell a burger on the grill. Gotta go!

Alternatives to Declawing

Instead of declawing your pet, why not take the time to direct your cat's natural scratching instinct to an appropriate place like a scratching post? Declawing is a painful and costly surgical procedure which removes the first joint of a cat's toe and its surrounding tissue. The recovery is painful and can be lengthy. There is a risk of infection, hemorrhage, or regrowth. Typically, only the front paws are declawed which leaves a cat dependent on her hind claws. Declawing leaves outdoor cats virtually defenseless against attack from other animals. If you adopt a cat who is already declawed, keep her indoors.

Some cats experience behavior changes such as biting and growling. Because of the pain and risk involved, many veterinarians will not perform this procedure. Britain and a few other countries have made declawing illegal.

Take time to show your cat which places she may scratch as well as correcting her when she scratches areas that are not acceptable. When you catch kitty scratching furniture, tell her "No," firmly and give her a quick squirt of water. Other suggestions include "hissing" at cat instead of using the firm "No". Or, you may want to try a shake can, an empty soft drink can with a few coins placed inside with the opening securely taped shut. Combine shaking the noisy can along with "No".

Provide Scratching Posts. Have a sturdy place for your cat to scratch. Make sure it is tall enough for her to scratch and is secured so it doesn't tip over. Scratching posts sprinkled with a little cat nip make the area even more inviting. After you catch kitty scratching where she shouldn't, direct her attention to the scratching post. Tantalize her with toys or yarn. When she scratches the post, reward your kitty with praise and a treat. Your cat will soon learn that scratching the couch leads to correction, but scratching the post leads to reward.

NOTE:
Declawing is a painful and costly procedure which removes the first joint of the cat's toes. It leaves cats defenseless. Please consider other options first.

Trim Claws. Keep your cat's claws trimmed and smooth. See GROOMING section for tips on trimming claws.

Don't Use Hands as Toys. By teasing kitty with your hands or fingers, you are training her to scratch and bite you.

Cover Nails. New plastic nail covers are now available to temporarily guard your family and furniture from scratches while you are training kitty to use her cat tree. These are similar to press-on nails for humans that can be applied by you or your veterinarian.

The Kitty Litter

When introducing a new kitten or cat to his litter box, use the same brand of litter that he's accustomed to. If you would like to use another brand, gradually mix litters over a period of time. An abrupt change in litter can send kitty looking for another place to relieve himself. Cats are darned serious about that litter. Don't mess around or they might too!

Litter Options

There are many different types of cat litters from which to choose, but ultimately the choice is kitty's. If he does not like the brand you've selected, urinating elsewhere is his veto. If this occurs, try other brands until he is satisfied.

Flushable. The benefits are obvious; you scoop, you drop, you flush. Simple as that.

Clumping. This litter clumps urine spots so you can scoop away easily. The drawback is that litter can stick to paws that cats will ingest while grooming. The possible health hazards from ingesting litter are still being debated. Some say that it is harmful while others contend that there is no danger to cat's health.

Scented. It may be tempting to use scented litters that mask the urine odor, but resist. Some scents such as citrus can repel cats. You don't want kitty to mistake her litter box for a fruit basket, or she'll need to search elsewhere to do her business.

Litter Boxes

Cats are finicky about everything and litter boxes are no exception. If your household box does not pass his inspection, guess how he lets you know? You got it -- he finds another place for his duties.

Scoop out litter box daily and always make sure the litter is fresh. Once a week, empty litter box and disinfect with bleach to prevent the breeding of germs that cause disease. Rinse thoroughly and leave outside to air out fumes. Avoid using pine-oil based products which are toxic to cats.

Each cat should have his own box. Large homes may require several boxes, placed strategically throughout the house so that kitty is never too far from an appropriate spot for relief. Be sure to place litter boxes in easily accessible areas that are not highly trafficked. Cats need their privacy.

Indoor Cats

On average, indoor cats live three times longer than outdoor cats. Cats love the outdoors. And why not? They can run free, climb trees, and chase birds. But for their own good, keep them inside. Although they are smart, quick, and alert, they cannot defend themselves against all the dangers of the outside world.

A cat can lead a happy fulfilling life indoors as long as you provide lots of love, attention, and, of course, toys. Inside your home, a cat is protected from:

NOTE:
On average, indoor cats live three times longer than outdoor cats.

- cars

- disease & parasites

- unsealed poisons

- unfriendly animals

- mean people

- traps

Chapter 11

Preventative Health Care

Wouldn't it be great if pets came with translating machines like the ones they use at the United Nations? You could place your earphones on and quickly understand that a certain high pitch meow means, "I have a lump in my ear that's causing me considerable pain." Since this nifty gadget doesn't exist, your pet depends on you to notice changes in health and seek veterinary care as needed.

In order to detect problems, you should become familiar with your pet's normal weight, behavior, and activity level. Notable changes in these areas should be a red flag that your pet is due for a trip to the veterinarian.

Inspect your pet's skin, eyes, ears, mouth, nose, paws, pads, and claws regularly. To make this more pleasurable for your pet, this can be done while petting or massaging the pet. The benefits of regular touching are three-fold. First, it will alert you early to any health problems; bumps, parasites, cuts, sores, or rashes. Second, it will help your pet become accustomed to being handled by people. And third, pets grow to enjoy the undivided attention. Have friends and family meet and handle your pets to help them become more comfortable with others. If the pet seems fearful or anxious, begin slowly by limiting the number of new people and the amount of time they spend with pet. Remember, the objective is to build up the pet's confidence, not to overwhelm him.

TIP: When setting your annual family budget, be sure to include regular veterinary care as well as unexpected medical costs.

Massaging your pet is a wonderful addition to your health maintenance routine. Once a week, give your pet a head-to-tail massage, gently moving both hands circularly around face, ears, neck, sides, legs, and feet. This helps your pet's circulation and directs your attention to any changes on skin surface.

While weekly massage is an excellent method of detecting problems, be sure to give your pet the sight and sniff test as well. Closely examine ears, smelling for irregular odor. If your pet scratches her ears or shakes her head, there may be a problem. Check with your veterinarian.

As your family sets its annual budget, be sure to include regular veterinary care as well as unexpected medical costs. Your best bet for a healthy pet is making sure her health care needs are met in a timely manner. Don't cut corners by using human medication, unless your veterinarian specifically advises this. It is a dangerous experiment that could even be deadly for your pet.

Take your pet on car trips that don't lead to the veterinarian to avoid anxiety around the car. This is more commonly known as *auto*phobia and can lead to many years of pet psychotherapy.

Finding the Right Veterinarian

The best way to find a veterinarian is to get a recommendation from someone you know and trust. If you are moving to a new city, ask your current veterinarian for a referral. You might also ask local animal welfare groups or shelters which local veterinarians volunteer their time. Doctors who provide free services to needy pets are likely to be in the profession for all the right reasons. Additionally, check medical societies and professional associations for membership as well as grievances or malpractice suits filed.

You may also contact the following groups for a listing of their members in your area.

Association of Veterinarians for Animal Rights
P.O. Box 208
Davis, CA 95617
916-759-8106

American Animal Hospital Association
P.O. Box 150899
Denver, CO 80215-0899
800-883-6301

When you visit a veterinarian's office, ask if you may tour the facility. Note the cleanliness of the facility both by sight and smell. Is the staff friendly and helpful? Do they seem to genuinely care for pets and people?

Are you comfortable with how the veterinarian or staff answers your questions? Or do you feel rushed and unimportant? Do the other pets seem at ease? Or are two cats plotting their escape from cell block C? Is the office conveniently located for you? What are the office hours? And what is the policy for emergencies during hours when the facility is closed? Do they offer grooming or boarding services?

For the Anxious Cat

As a rule, a cat's hatred of car rides is second only to her hatred of veterinarian visits. Nonetheless, you should take her on short trips in her cat carrier to other places to help kitty get used to the car. Think of it as a vet drill. The more you practice, the less stressful a real trip to the veterinarian will seem.

If your pet is especially nervous about trips to the veterinarian, you may consider going during slower times (ask appointment scheduler), taking kitty to a cats-only veterinarian, or finding a veterinarian who makes house calls.

Alternative Medicine

Similar to human medicine, many pet owners are seeking alternative methods of care outside of traditional medicine. Some seek this out for ongoing, preventative care. Others go in search as a last resort.

When traditional medicine offers no hope of helping their beloved pet, many pet owners seek the assistance of an alternative health practitioner. If alternative medicine is unable to cure the pet, it may at least provide pain relief, improving the pet's quality of life. This approach may be used independent of or in conjunction with traditional veterinary care.

NOTE: Holistic medicine treats the whole patient rather than just focusing on the area of discomfort. It may be used independent of or in conjunction with traditional care.

Holistic medicine treats the whole patient rather than just focusing on the area of discomfort. Body parts are not isolated, but instead seen as part of the entire living being. The veterinarian will try to determine what is going on in the pet's body as well as the pet's environment.

Less enlightened pets may tease yours and call her granola kitty, but holistic medicine is a well-respected and popular practice in most parts of the world. Some alternatives to traditional veterinary care include acupuncture, Bach flower remedies, basic and therapeutic nutrition, herbs, laser therapy, massage, homeopathy, magnetic therapy, and chiropractic care.

For more information or to locate a holistic practitioner in your area, send a SASE (Self-Addressed Stamped Envelope) to the following contacts:

American Holistic Veterinary Medicine Association
2214 Old Emmorton Road
Bel Air, MD 21015
410-569-0795

American Veterinary Chiropractic Association
P.O. Box 249
Port Byron, IL 61275
309-523-3995

International Veterinary Acupuncture Society
2140 Conestoga Road
Chester Springs, PA 19425
610-827-7245

International Association for Veterinary Homeopathy
334 Knollwood Lane
Woodstock, GA 30188
770-516-5954

Academy for Veterinary Homeopathy
1283 Lincoln Street
Eugene, OR 97401
503-342-7665

National Centre for Homeopathy
801 N. Fairfax St., Suite 306
Alexandria, VA 22314
703-548-7790

Preventative Care

The key to good health care, alternative or traditional, is prevention and early intervention. Vaccinations and parasite control will prevent contagious or fatal diseases. Weekly handling and thorough inspection of eyes, ears, feet, skin, teeth, and paws will alert you to potential problems. If you notice sudden change in pet's weight, appetite, or overall demeanor, let your veterinarian know immediately.

NOTE: Prevention and early intervention is the key to good health care, traditional or alternative.

Cats and dogs, like humans, can be protected by vaccination against many serious and potentially fatal diseases caused by bacteria and viruses.

Your veterinarian is your best source of advice regarding vaccinations and overall health of your pet. However, you are also an important source of information for your veterinarian. Be sure to tell your veterinarian about any special considerations that may have an effect on your pet's ability to respond to vaccines. These special circumstances could include stressful events, such as long car trips, exposure to sick animals, and changes in diet, sleeping, elimination, or other habits. Knowledge of these special circumstances, combined with a thorough examination of your pet, will help your veterinarian give your pet the best possible care.

According to the American Veterinary Medical Association, the following vaccinations are recommended for dogs and cats.

Recommended Canine Vaccinations

Recommended Canine Vaccinations

Date	DHLP*	Parvovirus	Bordatellosis	Rabies	Coronavirus

*Distemper, Hepatitis, Leptospirosis, Parainfluenza

Canine Diseases

Canine Distemper

This is a highly contagious viral disease transmitted by direct or indirect contact with the discharges from an infected dog's eyes or nose. A healthy dog does not need to come in direct contact with an infected dog because the virus can be carried by air currents and inanimate objects.

Early signs of canine distemper are similar to those of a severe cold and often go unrecognized by the pet owner. The respiratory problems may be accompanied by vomiting and diarrhea. A nervous system disorder may also develop. The death rate from canine distemper is greater than 50% in adult dogs and much higher in puppies. Even if the dog survives, distemper can cause permanent damage to a dog's nervous system, sense of smell, hearing, and sight. Partial or total paralysis is not uncommon.

Infectious Canine Hepatitis

This is caused by a virus that can infect many tissues, but usually attacks the liver causing hepatitis. In some instances, a whiteness or cloudiness of the eye may accompany the disease. Another strain of the same virus can cause respiratory tract infections. These viruses are transmitted by contact with objects that have been contaminated with the urine from infected dogs. Infectious Hepatitis is different from human hepatitis.

Canine Leptospirosis

This is a bacterial disease that impairs renal (kidney) function and may result in kidney failure. Clinical signs include vomiting, impaired vision, and convulsions. The disease is transmitted by contact with objects that have been contaminated with the urine of infected animals.

Canine Parainfluenza

This is caused by a virus which produces a mild respiratory tract infection. It is often associated with other respiratory tract viruses. In combination, these viruses are usually transmitted by contact with the nasal secretions of infected dogs.

Canine Parvovirus (CPV)

This is a serious problem due to the highly resistant nature of the virus. CPV can withstand extreme temperature changes and exposure to most disinfectants. The source of the infection is usually dog feces which can contaminate cages, shoes, and can be carried on the feet and hair of infected animals.

This virus attacks the intestinal tract, white blood cells, and heart muscle. Clinical signs include vomiting, severe diarrhea, accompanied by a loss of appetite, depression, and high fever. Most deaths occur within 48-72 hours after the onset of clinical signs. Pups, less than 3 months of age, can experience an inflammation of the heart (myocarditis). Infected pups may act depressed, collapse gasping for breath, and death may follow immediately. Pups that survive are likely to have permanently damaged hearts.

Canine Bordetellosis

This is caused by bacterium Bordetella Bronchiseptica which is present in the respiratory tracts of many animals. It is a primary cause of the severe chronic cough, tracheobronchitis (kennel cough). In addition to the cough, some dogs develop a purulent nasal discharge. Transmission most frequently occurs by contact with the nasal secretions of infected dogs.

Rabies

This viral disease can attack the central nervous system of all warm blooded animals, including humans. Once infected, the disease is fatal. In most parts of the United States both dog and cat owners are legally required to have their pets vaccinated against rabies. The disease is transmitted by saliva, which is usually transferred by a bite from an infected animal. The disease is commonly found in wild animals, such as skunks, foxes, raccoons, and bats.

Rabies is dangerous, deadly, but mostly totally preventable by vaccinations. Dogs and Cats should receive an initial vaccination at 3-4 months of age with regular boosters.

See next page for recommended cat vaccinations.....

Recommended Cat Vaccinations

Recommended Feline Vaccinations

Date	FVR-CP*	Pneumonitis (Chlamydiosis)	Rabies	Feline Leukemia

*Feline Viral Rhinotracheites, Claicivirus, Panleukopia (Feline Distemper)

Feline Diseases

Feline Panleukopenia

This is also known as feline infectious enteritis and feline distemper. This disease is caused by a resistant virus that may remain infectious for more than a year at room temperature on inanimate objects. It is transmitted through blood, urine, feces, and nasal secretions, and even by fleas from infected cats. The disease destroys many of the cat's white blood cells. The disease is fatal for 50% to 70% of the cats that have it. Cats with feline panleukopenia seem lethargic, vomit, have a high fever, and are dehydrated. Sickness may go on 3 to 4 days after the first signs are noticed and before death occurs.

Feline Viral Rhinotracheitis, Feline Calicivirus, and Feline Pneumonitis

These are diseases of the respiratory tract of cats. Infected animals are highly contagious to other cats and may show either acute or chronic respiratory signs.

Rabies

This viral disease can attack the central nervous system of all warm blooded animals, including humans. Once infected, the disease is fatal. In most parts of the United States both dog and cat owners are legally required to have their pets vaccinated against rabies. The disease is transmitted by saliva, which is usually transferred by a bite from an infected animal. The disease is commonly found in wild animals, such as skunks, foxes, raccoons, and bats.

Rabies is dangerous, deadly, but mostly totally preventable by vaccinations. Dogs and Cats should receive an initial vaccination at 3-4 months of age with regular boosters.

Feline Leukemia Virus

This is usually a fatal disease affecting the cat's immune system. This increases susceptibility to other diseases as well as leukemia. Signs of feline leukemia virus include weight loss, recurring or chronic illness, lethargy, fever, diarrhea, unusual breathing patterns, and a yellow color around the mouth and the whites of the eyes.

Warning Signs

Checking your pet on a weekly basis is the key to early detection or prevention of health problems. If eyes, ears, teeth, mouth, nose, feet and skin seem in good shape, terrific! But be aware of other warning signs to your pet's ill health.

NOTE:
If your pet seems aloof, not himself or uninterested in spending time with the family - call your veterinarian.

If he suddenly seems aloof, not himself or uninterested in

spending time with the family, talk to your veterinarian. Other dramatic changes in behavior such as whining, hiding, or urinating in the house may be symptoms of a bigger problem. Early intervention can prevent more serious conditions, so don't delay your visit to the veterinarian.

The following are warning signs of potential problems with pet's health. If you spot any of these warning signs, call your veterinarian.

Changes in Appetite or Weight

- Abnormal increase or decrease in appetite or weight
- Pet seems excessively thirsty

Vomiting

- Is especially a cause for concern if vomit has blood or bile in it. Cats are curious rascals and often eats things they shouldn't like string or rubber bands. Usually, they throw up these foreign objects later. If you catch kitty in the act, do not pull things out of her mouth. This may do more damage than good by harming kitty's intestines. Instead, call your veterinarian for advice.
- Note: Cat Hair balls. One of the most common causes for kitty vomiting is hair balls. This may be prevented by brushing your cat more frequently. This will reduce the amount of hair that she may swallow during her grooming sessions. Another way to help your cat is to regularly put a little petroleum jelly or butter on her paw for her to lick off. Be sure to rub it in a bit or kitty will butter the room.

Changes in Teeth

- Loss of teeth, tartar build-up, bad breath, pale or bleeding gums

Changes in Excretion

- Diarrhea or constipation that lasts over 24 hours or contains blood or mucous
- Increased urination, "accidents," difficulty urinating and passing little or no urine, urine that contains blood or is cloudy

Abnormal Discharge
- From eyes, ears, or nose

Changes in Fur
- Balding in spots or coat becoming ragged and dull

Skin Irritations
- Dry, flaking, skin
- Patches of red or inflamed skin, sores or irritations

Coughing or Heavy Breathing
- Coughing, sneezing, excessive panting, shortness of breath or difficulty breathing

Limping
- Limping on any leg, reluctance to move, difficulty getting up or down

Scooting
- Dragging bottom on floor

Scratching
- Head shaking, excessive scratching, licking or biting one particular area

Lumps
- Bumps, lumps, or growths on or under surface of skin

Behavior Changes
- Sudden viciousness, lethargy, hiding, or a change in sleeping patterns or position

Spaying and Neutering

Let's face it, cats and dogs just aren't ready for contraception. They forget to take their pills and think condoms are chew toys. So it's up to us humans to help control the epidemic pet overpopulation problem by having pets spayed or neutered.

NOTE:
Over 12 million abandoned cats and dogs are destroyed each year. Sterilizing cats and dogs is the only responsible choice.

Every year, over 12 million abandoned cats and dogs are destroyed. Sterilizing cats and dogs is the only responsible choice.

Spaying Females

Rather than incur the responsibility of caring for unplanned puppies or kittens and the difficult task of finding them good homes, have your female pet spayed. Spaying your cat or dog improves her general well-being, greatly reduces the risk of breast cancer, and eliminates uterine infections. A spayed female is also less likely to roam or have male suitors spraying on your property.

Neutering Males

Neutering your male pet will reduce sexual frustration, prostate problems, and may help curb other behavior problems like aggression, mounting, and spraying. Additionally, a neutered male is less likely to stray, decreasing his chances of getting lost, hurt, or killed.

Contact the following group for information on low-cost spaying and neutering services:

■ SPAY/USA   800-248-SPAY

Dental Care

Think about how much you enjoy dental visits and care. Okay, your pet will probably enjoy it even less. Not only do pets and humans have a distaste for dental care in common, we also share a real need for this preventive care. Regular dental care, like tooth brushing, dental chews, and cleanings by a veterinarian can prevent tooth loss, gum inflammation, and pain.

Brushing Pet's Teeth

Pets will probably never like having their teeth brushed. If necessary, you may need to restrain your pet in a towel or pet handling bag. Be sensitive to the fact that this is a frightening experience.

Let your pet get used to you checking inside her mouth by gently lifting one lip at a time. After a few inspections, she'll become more comfortable and less resistant to this. Then, touch pet's teeth with your finger and gently massage the teeth. Begin with the outside of the teeth, then massage in back as well. Do this every day for a few days until she seems tolerant of the process. Now, you are ready to move on to a finger brush or a pet toothbrush. You have mastered the art of pet dental care when you begin using pet toothpaste. Do not use human toothpaste or baking soda.

Avoiding Plaque and Tartar

Brushing pet's teeth is a must for avoiding plaque and tartar, but other precautionary steps may be taken as well. Have your veterinarian regularly check teeth and schedule cleanings when necessary. Feed your pet hard, dry food and give her chew toys designed to remove plaque such as rawhide and nubby Nylabone® chews.

Warning Signs of Dental Problems

Despite our best efforts, sometimes our pets have dental problems anyway. Preventive care will minimize the occurrence, but be on the lookout for signs of trouble. The sooner you detect a problem, the sooner you can get your pet proper care.

As you inspect your pet's mouth, check for swollen gums or cheeks, accumulation of tartar, sores, or pale gums. If your pet seems unusually reluctant to open his mouth, it could be because of dental problems. When he finally opens his mouth, a case of bad breathe could be a trouble sign.

As you observe your pet in his daily activities, you may notice that he seems reluctant to eat or seems to be uncomfortable when he does. If he drools excessively or has blood in his saliva, it's time for a trip to the veterinarian for a dental checkup.

Parasites

Pets can be attacked by a variety of internal and external parasites. Once again, prevention is the key, have your pet regularly checked. If you suspect worms, contact your veterinarian. If possible, plan on bringing a stool sample to your veterinarian for analysis.

Internal Parasites: Worms

Hookworm - Named for their hook-shaped teeth, these worms attach themselves to pet's intestinal lining and feed on their blood. Nice, huh? Hookworm can be fatal to puppies and kittens. So, if your pet seems lethargic, has a loss of appetite, or excretes a black, tarry stool, don't delay taking your pet to the veterinarian. Bring a stool sample for the doctor to analyze as well.

Roundworm - Virtually all pets are born with this common parasite or get it while nursing. Older pets can contract roundworm during normal contact with soil infected by tiny roundworm eggs. Symptoms of roundworm are diarrhea and vomiting, bloated stomach, and a rough coat. Take pet and stool samples to the veterinarian.

Tapeworm - These little critters sneak into your pet's body through his digestive track. A swallowed flea or infested animal, typically a rodent, can be a vehicle for worms. Symptoms are more subtle, but parts of the worm can be seen in an infected pet's stool. Take pet and a stool sample to the veterinarian.

For Dogs Only

Heartworm - Living in the heart of a dog, these parasites are the most life-threatening. They stress a dog's heart which restricts blood flow to the organs and may cause failure, possibly leading to death. Keeping in mind that heartworm is easy to prevent and difficult to cure, ask your veterinarian to test your dog for heartworm and prescribe preventive medication. Because heartworm plugs the heart of a dog, it impairs proper circulation. Symptoms of heartworm may be weight loss, lethargy, and poor endurance. Other warning signs of heartworm include exercise intolerance, labored breathing, and coughing.

Whipworm - These little buggers obviously never heard the age-old real estate adage: location, location, location. They choose to make their home at the lower end of a pet's digestive tract. Preventive vaccines are key because whipworm is difficult to detect and evict. Some clues that your dog has whipworm will be chronic bowel inflammation, diarrhea, weight loss, and dehydration.

Tips for Preventing Worm Infestation:

- Keep pet away from soil contaminated with animal feces. (Parasites can transmit their eggs to pets who sniff or come into contact with infected fecal matter.)
- Stop pet from eating wildlife.
- Groom regularly (keep flea-free).
- Keep bedding clean.
- Have veterinarian check for worms regularly.

External Parasites: Fleas, Ticks, & Mites

Fleas

The scratching, the itching, the stinging - it's driving you and your pet nuts! Fleas are more than just irritating pests, they're the enemy. It's time to declare WAR. Combatting fleas will be an ongoing effort on your part. Without a long-term strategy, fleas will return and bring their friends.

If yours is an outdoor pet or if visitors have flea problems, eliminating fleas all together is nearly impossible. At best, you may be able to control them.

How to Detect a Flea Problem

If your pet is scratching himself often, you may have a flea problem. Comb pet with a flea comb and see if you catch any. They are tiny, dark bugs about the size of a grain of sand. If you have fleas, they will leave "flea dirt," which looks like black specks in your pet's fur. Flea dirt is typically found on a pet's back, tail, groin, or hindquarters area. Flea dirt may also be found where the pet sleeps.

NOTE: Unlike most parasites, fleas tend to spend more time off your pet. 95% of your flea problem will be in your house and yard.

Fleas do not make a permanent home on your pet. Unlike internal parasites, they love to travel and spend a great deal of time off your pet's body. In fact, 95% of your flea problem will be in your house and yard so it's important to treat the environment as well as the pet. Eliminating fleas requires a three-step plan. You must treat your pet, home, and yard to be effective.

De-Flea Your Pet

Using flea or citrus shampoo, bathe pets weekly. Between baths, comb pets with a flea comb and use powders or sprays designed to eliminate fleas. Add garlic or vinegar to your pet's food. Think about it, if you were a flea, would you want to drink blood spiked with garlic or vinegar? You might also give your pet an aloe vera drink to relieve skin irritation. After fleas are gone, your pet may still itch from previously irritated skin. Ask your veterinarian about shampoos that will relieve skin irritations.

Talk with your veterinarian about safe new products on the market designed for flea control. Many of these new products are only available through your veterinarian.

De-Flea Your Home

Wash all of your pet's bedding, slipcovers, throw rugs, and coverings weekly. Vacuum and sweep twice weekly and dispose of vacuum bags immediately.

Treat your entire home with a flea control product. Make sure you apply flea treatment everywhere, behind appliances, under cushions, under furniture, and especially the places your pet likes to hang out. A cedar chip bed for your pet may repel fleas from the area.

De-Flea Your Yard

Remove food, water bowls, and toys from yard before treating area. Concentrate on treating moist areas and places where your pet spends a lot of time. Some flea treatment products can be dispersed using a sprayer connected to your water hose. Diatomaceous earth or pyrethrum dust are considered natural alternative treatments, or you can try nematodes, insects that attack and destroy flea larvae. These bugs are reportedly harmless to other bugs, birds, and animals.

Flea Maintenance

For a week or two after treating your yard, you may notice an increase in flea activity. Don't worry, this is normal. Flea pupae is impossible to kill and vacuuming or other activity may actually stimulate hatching. These young fleas will soon meet their demise by flea treatment residual left in your house, on your yard, and on your pet.

Congratulate yourself for a job well done, but remember that regular maintenance is essential to keeping fleas under control. Even when you don't see fleas, keep up the shampooing and treatments. Consult your veterinarian on flea control and ask which products she recommends. To avoid adverse reactions from incompatible products, consult your veterinarian before combining products.

Good luck! And for the sake of your family and pet's comfort, be persistent in your routine.

Ticks and Mites

Just when you thought it was safe to keep reading, just when you thought all discussion of creepy, crawly, wiggly parasites was over, just when you thought you'd heard it all, there's one more group of parasites to learn about: ticks and mites. However unsettling this is for you, it is important to fully understand what pets are up against. Your pet's best defense against disease and parasites is an educated owner, so hang in there.

Ticks

Pets typically pick up ticks during outdoor excursions. Check pet's skin regularly for ticks. A number of diseases are transmitted via tick bites.

Tick Removal

Use tweezers to remove the tick from your pet's body. Be sure to get the whole tick, leaving a part behind could cause sores and infection. Avoid directly handling the tick if possible by using tissue or latex gloves. Afterwards, wash hands thoroughly. Dab hydrogen peroxide or rubbing alcohol on the area to prevent infection. Tick removal tools are available.

Ear Mites

Ear mites look like dark, granular substance in your pet's ears. Don't dismiss it as dirt. Left untreated, ear mites can cause hearing loss. If pet shakes his head or scratches his ears with paws, talk to your veterinarian.

Pet Nutrition

Another thing pets and humans have in common is a need for a balanced diet. Proper nutrition is critical to your pet's health and well-being.

Premium Pet Food

Premium pet food can be more expensive, yet at the same time more economical. Allow us to explain. Nutrients in premium food are more concentrated and are absorbed better by pets. Therefore, you use less food than you'd have to with a cheaper brand. Say you've got Primo Dog Chow which costs $10 and lasts your pooch two weeks, and Cheapo Brand Dog Food which costs $7, but only lasts five days. The more expensive food is actually the better deal. It tastes great, and is more filling. Does your pet deserve any less? And let's not forget the benefits to you - more absorption by pet equals less poop.

Nutrition Needs

Manufacturers offer foods that meet specific nutritional needs of pets in certain age or size classifications. For instance, you wouldn't want to feed your active, growing puppy the same food as you would Grandpa Lassie. Choose the food that meets your pet's age and activity level (Puppy, Kitten, Adult, Active, Inactive, Senior).

Feeding Tips

Each pet should have his own food dish, set at least three feet apart from the next closest pet bowl. If your pet is tall, elevate the bowl so he doesn't have to strain to reach it. Only use food supplements if your veterinarian recommends it.

NOTE: People food does not meet the nutritional needs of a pet and adds additional calories to their diet. Choose a food that fits your pet's age and activity level.

People food is generally a bad idea for pets because it does not meet their nutritional needs and adds unnecessary calories to their diet. If you absolutely can't resist sharing your food with a begging pet, limit table scraps to no more than 10% of pet's diet. Put scraps in pet's bowl or a pet will become your shadow at the table. Pets who are rewarded for begging can become a nuisance, especially to guests who want to enjoy their meal without a guilt trip from Miss Kitty.

Never feed a pet chocolate or onions. Bones can also be dangerous for a pet. Before giving your pet any bones, please talk with your veterinarian first.

Select nutritious snacks for your pet that can be given as treats during training or between meals. Fresh fruit and vegetables like carrots, apples, and grapes make great snacks. Give your pets snacks sparingly and never use as a replacement for regular meals.

Feeding A Cat

There are basically three options for a cat's feeding schedule:

1) **Like Clockwork** - Feed cat at same time each day. After a set time, remove the food bowl and any leftovers.

2) **Measured Feeding** - Allow only a certain amount of food to be placed in a bowl which kitty has access to all day.

3) **Bottomless Bowl** - Fill cat bowl whenever it's empty.
   Just keep that food coming, regardless of time of day or amount she's already eaten. This feeding method is not a good idea for overweight cats.

C a t

TIP:
To slow down an overzealous eater, put small, clean, one-to-two inch rocks in the food bowl. Your cat will have to slow down to pick the food out of the rocks.

Grass: Some cats enjoy nibbling on grass and it's okay. You may want to grow grass specifically for your kitty, this may keep her out of your other houseplants. Don't use grass seeds that are dyed or have been chemically treated.

Don't: Feed your cat dog food.

It doesn't contain the right balance of nutrients for a cat.

Do: Use caution when giving milk to adult cats, many are lactose intolerant and will get diarrhea.

Feeding a Dog

Schedule regular meal times for your dog which last about 30 minutes before you remove the food bowl. Always keep fresh water available for your pooch. If you change pet food, gradually mix old and new food. This gives your dog a chance to get used to the new food and minimizes digestive upsets which may result in diarrhea. Once you find a brand both you and your dog are happy with, stick with it. Avoid feeding an hour before or after rigorous activity.

Obesity

Pets have no vanity. They're not going to check themselves out in the mirror, realize swim suit season is fast-approaching, and high-tail it over to gym. It's up to you to be your pet's weight watcher.

When you place your hands on your pet's rib cage, do you feel his ribs? Or do you dig through a sea of blubber to find them? Does his rib cage seem lost all together? Has your pet lost his waist? Does that "tuck up" seem tuckered out? If you answered "yes" to any of the last four questions, you've been overfeeding your pet. It's time to begin a weight-loss regiment.

Excess weight and obesity is not only uncomfortable for your pet, it's unhealthy. Obese pets may fatigue easily, lack energy, stress joints, and be less mobile. Overweight pets are also more prone to injury and increase stress on vital organs such as their heart, lungs, liver, and kidneys. If your pet should need surgery, excess weight will increase the health risks.

Trimming Down Your Chubby Buddy

Talk to your veterinarian about how to safely trim down an overweight pet. She can offer diet and exercise tips for your fat cat or round hound. She may suggest decreasing food portions or switching pet food to one that is low in fat.

Exercise will be necessary. Talk with your veterinarian about your pet's health. She will have advice on what amount of exercise is reasonable for your pet. Begin slowly and gradually increase your pet's activity. As your pet establishes this new lifestyle, you will notice a renewed, happier, and more energetic pet emerging. Your pet will also enjoy the additional active time and attention he will receive from you as you participate in his exercise program.

If you want to feed your dog snacks, make sure that they are low fat snacks such as carrots, oranges, apples, seedless grapes, bananas, pretzels, or unbuttered popcorn.

Care and Handling Tips

Giving a Cat a Pill

Never give a pet human medication unless your veterinarian approves. It could be harmful to your pet. If you must give your cat a pill, you might try a specially designed pill plunger. Or you could hide the pill in pureed baby food or her favorite moist cat food. Make sure she actually eats the pill instead of maneuvering her way around it.

NOTE: Never give a pet human medication unless advised by your veterinarian. It could be very harmful to your pet.

The following is the direct approach of depositing pills into a cat's mouth. It may sound complicated, but it's really not. Try acting it out with an imaginary cat as you read, you'll realize it's actually quite simple.

- Butter the pill to make it slippery.
- Sit on the floor, bend open legs with feet together, creating a diamond shaped border in which to place

the cat.

- Back your cat's legs into your body.
- Gently open kitty's mouth by applying slight pressure on short teeth (right behind their "fangs").
- Drop pill as far back into the throat as possible.
- Close mouth, tip head gently up.
- Softly stroke throat from top to bottom to encourage swallowing.
- Mission accomplished when you feel the gulp of the swallowed pill.

Don't Let the Cat Outta the Bag

When giving cats pills, baths, or when grooming, you may find it helpful to wrap kitty in a towel to inhibit her movement and prevent scratching. You may also purchase a special cat handling bag for this purpose. Whether using a cat bag or towel, make sure all four legs and paws are secured and kitty's head is sticking out.

Giving a Dog a Pill

When giving your dog a pill, try hiding it in his food and sprinkling it with onion powder. As with cats, make sure your dog has eaten the pill, not just shuffled it around from one side of the bowl to the other. To insert a pill directly into your dog's mouth, lubricate it with a little butter first. Then tilt his head back, place pill on back of tongue, remove your fingers and close dog's mouth. Rub throat gently to induce swallowing. If your veterinarian approves, reward your brave friend with a treat.

Chapter 12

Grooming

Grooming is a necessary part of your pet's care so have fun with it! Your attitude and approach to grooming will set the tone. Having a good attitude, patience, and a smile will help put your pet at ease. Many pets enjoy grooming (well, at least the brushing part). This is their one-on-one time with you, where they get your undivided attention. So, relax, laugh, and praise your pet for his grooming tolerance.

Regular grooming keeps your cats and dogs feeling, looking, and smelling their best. It can also offer valuable insights into your pet's health and well-being. A grooming session should include brushing, checking ears, eyes, feet and teeth, bathing (if needed), hair clipping for some pets, and a delicious treat for being such a good sport (that's for the pet, not you).

Benefits of Grooming

Regular grooming stimulates circulation and distributes oils, helping your pet maintain a beautiful coat and healthy skin. This routine handling can also alert pet parents to any possible parasite, skin, or medical problems early on.

The Grooming Process

Begin grooming immediately with short, enjoyable sessions. Slowly accustom pet to the grooming routine. Establish a routine and groom systematically so your pet knows what to expect. Start with their head and back, then gradually add their tail, legs, and their sensitive tummy. Keep the sessions short in the beginning and lavish pet with praise and a treat at the end of the session. Remember to keep it fun!

NOTE: Grooming stimulates circulation and distributes oils, helping your pet maintain a beautiful coat and healthy skin.

Begin With Brushing

Types of Brush

Brushing your pet's coat is a good place to start. But, before you can begin, you must have the right grooming tools. Tools are available for all types of fur. If you have a short hair pet, soft or medium bristle brushes work well. Rubber mitts also work well for removing dead hair and redistributing oils. For long coats, you will need a comb to gently work out tangles and follow with a long bristle brush. If your pet has a double coat, then a slicker brush or rake comb is needed. If you are unsure as to which grooming tools you need, ask your veterinarian or a groomer for their advice.

Tangles

Remove tangles with fingers or a wide-toothed comb. For your pet's comfort, avoid pulling or yanking on hair, it hurts.

There are special combs available for those tough knots.

Brushing

When brushing, use short gentle strokes and work a small area at a time. Brush with, not against, the natural direction of hair. Remember, you're not styling or teasing puppy's hair for a night on the town.

Clean Eyes & Ears

Dampen a cotton ball, wash cloth, or tissue to wipe eyes. Gently wipe from inside corner to outside. Use new cloth on each eye to avoid spreading of possible contaminants. Use warm water to make this as comfortable for your pet as possible.

Wipe pet's ears with a warm, wet washcloth or cotton ball. Use a fresh wipe for each ear to avoid spreading germs. Don't use cotton swabs, they may push wax into the ear. If your pet has excessive ear wax, redness, or has an odor, contact your veterinarian. This may be a symptom of a medical problem.

Paw Care

Neglected nails can be painful to pet and harmful to others. Additionally, overgrown nails can cause damage to home and clothing. Check nails weekly and trim as necessary. Don't forget about those dewclaws (the "thumb" that's a little higher than the other four). Use this opportunity to inspect paws and pads for pebbles, foxtail grass, or any other foreign objects.

For new pet owners, you may want to ask your veterinarian or groomer to demonstrate how to trim nails first. This is probably the least favorite grooming ritual for your pet because if you trim too short, it is painful.

The idea is to keep your pet's nails at a comfortable length. Too short or too long is not comfortable. Slowly trim each nail from top to bottom, rather than from side to side which can pinch. Be careful not to cut into the "quick" which hurts and will bleed. The quick looks like a shadow of the nail inside it. It may be red or have a pinkish color. It is living tissue and your pet will experience pain if it is cut. After trimming, be sure to file the nail to smooth rough edges and prevent injury to you, your pet, or your furnishings.

If you accidentally cut the quick, stop the bleeding with styptic powder, flour, or cornstarch. This may sting a bit.

Bathing

Cats typically do not need, and especially don't want you to bathe them. They groom themselves and only need to be bathed if they have a flea or tick problem, special allergies, gotten into a messy situation (junior spilled his chocolate milk on Miss Kitty), or aren't properly grooming themselves.

Dogs usually aren't crazy about baths either. And, just like cats, they should only be bathed when they have flea or tick problems, skin allergies, or are just dirty. Keep in mind that bathing too frequently is not good for a dog. It robs his skin of essential oils and can leave him with dry, itchy, sensitive skin. And sometimes when your dog is a bit, shall we say, malodorous, it does not mean he needs a bath. Dogs with clean coats can smell bad because of dirty ears or teeth, or full anal glands. So, a bath wouldn't solve your smelly dog dilemma.

Preparing for Pet's Bath

- Accept the fact that you will be getting wet and dress accordingly.
- For pet's stability, place a rubber mat or towel in the sink or bathtub.
- Have your towels, pet shampoo, and tub ready.
- Use warm water at a comfortable temperature.
- Be sure pet can fit into sink or bathtub.
- Brush pet's coat and trim nails before bath.
- Put cotton balls in ears to prevent soap and water from getting in.

Bath Time

Begin washing your pet's head and face with a damp wash-cloth, carefully avoiding eyes and ears. For pets with fleas, before getting your pet wet, start by applying a ring of shampoo around your pet's neck. This will stop fleas from rushing to your pet's head for safety. Remember, this is an unnatural and scary experience for a pet. Use a soothing voice, reassure them that everything is okay. If your pet has a clean head and face and seems upset when this area is washed, you may consider skipping it and begin your shampooing at the neck.

Be sure you are using pet shampoo, the PH in human shampoo is too harsh for pets and can leave skin dry and flaky. A spray attachment can make rinsing much simpler. Whatever your method of rinsing your pet, be careful of spraying or pouring water in pet's face. First of all, they don't like it and secondly, you want to avoid getting shampoo in their eyes, nose, or mouth. Work from head down to the neck, then move on to body and legs. Rinse well. Then rinse again. It is important to get all the shampoo out of pet's coat.

NOTE:
Bathing too frequently is not good for your pet. It robs the skin of essential oils and can leave him with dry, itchy, sensitive skin.

After the Bath

- Towel dry (most pets are so relieved to get out of the sink or tub that they seem to like the toweling off).
- You can try blow drying hair on a low setting. (If pet seems too upset, stop.)
- Keep dryer moving and at least six inches away from pet to avoid burning.
- Keep pet in a draft-free area until dry.
- Give a final brush to remove remaining loose hair.
- On cold weather days keep pet indoors until he's completely dry.
- If it is a warm day outside, you may consider bathing your pet by hose, in a tub, or wading pool in the yard. When whether permits, air or towel drying will do, but if you

want to keep your pet clean, do not let him loose in the
yard while damp.

Clipping & Trimming

If She Don't Look Good, You Don't Look Good

While your dog need not sport the trendiest new hair cut,
you'll want to trim and clip his coat for pet's comfort and
protection. Talk to a groomer about hair cuts for your breed.
Even if you sport a military buzz cut for yourself, don't trim
your pet's hair too close to the skin. It won't give Private
Pugsly any more discipline, and his hair serves the function
of protecting him from sun exposure, insect bites, and skin
injuries.

Professional Groomers

You may decide to use a professional groomer. A groomer
will trim your dog's nails, clean ears and eyes, brush, bathe,
and cut hair according to breed specifications. In most com-
munities, you have a choice of mobile groomers or grooming
shops. Mobile groomers are an excellent option for pets that
don't travel well, have health concerns, or special needs. The
pets are groomed in the mobile groomers facilities (typically
a van) just outside the pet owner's home. This option offers
several advantages.

- No dropping or picking pet up
- No exposure to other pets, reducing health risks
- Comfort of family members presence
- Limited time with groomer
- May be less stressful to pet

Whether you choose a grooming shop or mobile groomer, use
the same care in selecting a groomer as you would in selecting a veterinarian. Ask others who they would recommend.
The following organizations can also provide groomer referrals.

American Grooming Shop Association
4575 Galley Road #400-A
Colorado Springs, CO 80915
719-570-7788 or 208-743-0153

National Dog Groomers Association of America
P.O. Box 101
Clark, PA 16113
412-962-2711

Questions to Ask

- What are his credentials?

- Is he certified?

- How long has he been in business?

- Will your dog be in contact with other pets?

- What grooming products will be used?

- What drying techniques are used?

- Can you tour the facility to check cleanliness and see how other pets are treated?

Whether you chose to have a professional groom your pet or you do it yourself, the important thing is that your pet is groomed regularly. With the right attitude, patience, and a sense of humor, you and your pet will enjoy the grooming process. And, most importantly, your pet will look and feel great.

Activity Notes:

Date: _____

_____
Name of Location

_____
City or Area

❑Park   ❑Trail   ❑Beach   ❑Other _____

What would you rate this location? _____
(1-Ho hum, 5-Great) Meaning - *Would you go back?*

Things we did: _____
_____
_____
_____
_____
_____
_____

Likes: _____
_____
_____
_____
_____
_____

Special Notes:
_____
_____
_____
_____
_____
_____
_____
_____
_____

Activity Notes: Date: _____

_____
Name of Location

_____
City or Area

❑Park   ❑Trail   ❑Beach   ❑Other _____

What would you rate this location? _____
(1-Ho hum, 5-Great) Meaning - *Would you go back?*

Things we did: _____
_____
_____
_____
_____
_____

Likes: _____
_____
_____
_____
_____
_____

Special
Notes:
_____
_____
_____
_____
_____
_____
_____
_____
_____

Activity Notes:

Date: _____

_____
Name of Location

_____
City or Area

❏Park   ❏Trail   ❏Beach   ❏Other _____

What would you rate this location? _____
(1-Ho hum, 5-Great) Meaning - *Would you go back?*

Things we did: _____
_____
_____
_____
_____
_____
_____

Likes: _____
_____
_____
_____
_____
_____

Special Notes:
_____
_____
_____
_____
_____
_____
_____
_____
_____
_____

Restaurant Notes: Date: _____

_____
Name of Restaurant

_____
City or Area

How would you rate the overall experience? _____
Food _____   Service _____   Pet-Friendly_____
 (1-Ho hum, 5-Great) Meaning - *Would you go back?*

What we ate:
_____
_____
_____
_____
_____
_____

Were there other pets there?
_____
_____
_____

Likes:
_____
_____
_____
_____
_____
_____
_____

Dislikes?
_____
_____
_____

Restaurant Notes: Date: _____

_____
Name of Restaurant

_____
City or Area

How would you rate the overall experience? _____
Food _____   Service _____   Pet-Friendly_____
(1-Ho hum, 5-Great) Meaning - *Would you go back?*

What we ate:
_____
_____
_____
_____
_____
_____

Were there other pets there?
_____
_____
_____

Likes:
_____
_____
_____
_____
_____
_____
_____
_____

Dislikes?
_____
_____
_____

Restaurant Notes: Date: _____

_____
Name of Restaurant

_____
City or Area

How would you rate the overall experience? _____
Food _____   Service _____   Pet-Friendly_____
(1-Ho hum, 5-Great) Meaning - *Would you go back?*

What we ate:
_____
_____
_____
_____
_____
_____

Were there other pets there?
_____
_____
_____

Likes:
_____
_____
_____
_____
_____
_____
_____

Dislikes?
_____
_____
_____